THE ED LEADERSHIP PLAYBOOK

THE ED LEADERSHIP PLAYBOOK

30 Lessons for Success

JARED R. SMITH, PhD

Copyrighted Material

The Ed Leadership Playbook
30 Lessons for Success

Copyright © 2024 by Dr. Jared Smith LLC. All Rights Reserved.

No part of this publication may be reproduced, stored in a retrieval system or transmitted, in any form or by any means—electronic, mechanical, photocopying, recording or otherwise—without prior written permission from the publisher, except for the inclusion of brief quotations in a review.

For information about this title or to order other books and/or electronic media, contact the publisher:

Dr. Jared Smith LLC
drjaredsmith.com
dr.jaredrsmith@gmail.com

ISBNs:
978-1-7372904-4-5 (print)

Printed in the United States of America

Cover and Interior design: 1106 Design

Please note that past performance may not be indicative of future results and does not guarantee any specific results or outcomes based on the use of the information provided in this book.

Thank you!

Table of Contents

Introduction	vii
LESSON 1: First Impressions Matter	1
LESSON 2: Lead with Integrity	9
LESSON 3: Ask Questions	16
LESSON 4: Not Knowing Is Okay	23
LESSON 5: Embrace Criticism	31
LESSON 6: Build Relationships with Staff	40
LESSON 7: Make Time for People	49
LESSON 8: Hold Frequent 1:1 Meetings	58
LESSON 9: Give All Employees a Voice	66
LESSON 10: Be Visible	75
LESSON 11: Leverage Social Media	83
LESSON 12: Utilize Effective Communication	90
LESSON 13: Collaborative Decision-Making	97
LESSON 14: Leading Change	103
LESSON 15: No Surprises	111

LESSON 16: Optimize Email	119
LESSON 17: Delegation	128
LESSON 18: Run Good Meetings	136
LESSON 19: Teacher Evaluation	143
LESSON 20: Employee Management	151
LESSON 21: Dealing with Toxic Staff	162
LESSON 22: Classroom Walkthroughs	169
LESSON 23: Trust Your Employees	177
LESSON 24: Treat Teachers As Professionals	185
LESSON 25: Invest in Culture	191
LESSON 26: Navigating a Teacher Shortage	202
LESSON 27: Staff Burnout	213
LESSON 28: The Gift of Time	223
LESSON 29: Handling Job Rejection	233
LESSON 30: Lack of Experience	241
BONUS LESSON: Growing Leaders	249
Conclusion	259
Looking for More?	261
About the Author	263
Thank You	265
Endnotes	267

Introduction

*"It's not whether you get knocked down;
it's whether you get back up."*

—Vince Lombardi

■ ■ ■

At age 12, I was introduced to the world of tackle football.

A rite of passage in most American middle schools, my classmates and I put on our pads and laced up our cleats for the very first time in seventh grade.

After weeks of practice, I was named the starting "A-Team" quarterback. While this position gained me a lot of prestige and popularity, it also came with significant responsibility.

Being the starting quarterback meant I had to master our team's playbook. To this day, I can still recall when my coach handed me a thick binder filled with diagrams and drawings. *"Whoa—an actual football playbook!"* I thought to myself. *"The only time I've seen one of these is on Nintendo!"*

Once the excitement wore off, reality set in. The sheer volume of information was overwhelming. *"Duuude! There's no way I'll remember all of this!"* I recall thinking.

But through studying and repetition, I began to familiarize myself with the playbook. Not only did I learn how our team needed to work together to execute each play, I began to understand the underlying principles of effective football.

Me. Before the broken arm (obviously).

Although my season was cut short after only two games as a result of a crushing hit by the massive middle linebacker from our crosstown rival, I began to understand the connection between having a dependable playbook and effective leadership.

In many ways, my experience as a young quarterback mirrors the challenges faced by educational leaders. Just as I was expected to fall back on a set of guidelines while directing our offense, school leaders must also fall back on a set of principles while leading their buildings.

The *Ed Leadership Playbook* outlines 30 principles for school leaders to consider as they create their own set of leadership fundamentals. From building relationships to leading change to running meetings, you will learn things that have worked—*and haven't worked*—while serving as an assistant principal, principal, and superintendent.

As you dive into the book, you'll find that these leadership principles aren't just theoretical concepts. Instead, they come to life through real-life anecdotes, making the concepts easy to grasp and apply. Furthermore, this book is firmly anchored in sound research, drawing wisdom from educational leaders and academic scholars.

What sets *The Ed Leadership Playbook* apart from other books is perspective. Let's be honest; most educational authors are far removed from the realities unfolding within our schools. They often write from a distant academic ivory tower, seemingly detached from the daily challenges faced by educators and leaders on the frontlines.

In contrast, this book is built upon the real-life experiences of a current educational leader with more than two decades of service in public education. As someone who operates deep in the trenches of an urban school district, you will hear a fresh and honest perspective about what *really* works in today's schools.

Before proceeding any further, you are encouraged to pick up a pen or pencil. Much like a football playbook, feel free to underline, circle, highlight, and jot down notes as you read. This will help you revisit key lessons without having to read the book again. After all, the purpose of books is not for them to remain untouched, but rather for the reader to extract the utmost value from each page.

At the end of each section, you'll discover a valuable opportunity for personal and professional growth. Engage with the material on a deeper level by exploring the reflective questions provided. Whether you choose to ponder these questions individually or as an administrative team, they are designed to deepen your understanding and application of the leadership strategies discussed.

Well . . . what are you waiting for? It's time to lace up your cleats and put on your shoulder pads. Whether you're a seasoned veteran or a wide-eyed rookie, let's huddle up and dive into these game-changing strategies for success on the educational leadership gridiron.

Lesson 1

First Impressions Matter

"I think self-awareness is probably the most important thing towards being a champion."

—Billie Jean King

※ ※ ※

First impressions matter.

While good first impressions can serve as the foundation for a strong relationship, bad first impressions are nearly impossible to undo.

For school leaders who assume a new position, few first impressions are more important than the opening-day speech. When I became a superintendent for the first time in 2018, I wanted to make my opening-day speech extra special. So, we took all 250 employees to a nearby convention center for a "Back-to-School Celebration" a week before school started.

As a relatively young superintendent (36 years old), I felt pressure to show I could effectively lead the district despite my age. Hoping to set a tone of competence and confidence, I crafted an introductory speech outlining my educational history, work accomplishments, leadership philosophy, and long-term goals.

The day before the celebration I met a mentor for lunch. During our conversation, he encouraged me to provide an overview of my introductory message. Eager for feedback, I summarized my speech, explaining my intent was to appear highly skilled and self-assured to compensate for my inexperience.

To my surprise, the mentor challenged my thinking. While he agreed there were solid aspects to the speech, he offered an alternate suggestion. Whereas most leaders believe introductions are a time to ooze confidence, he proposed I utilize a more down-to-earth approach.

"Don't forget to show them you're human," he advised. *"Vulnerability isn't a bad thing."*

That night I barely slept. Already anxious for the following day, the mentor's advice to modify the message did nothing to calm my fears.

"Vulnerability . . . the first time I meet these people?" I thought while lying in bed. *"I'm not sure that's a good idea."*

※ ※ ※

The next morning, I woke up feeling more receptive to the mentor's recommendation. I updated the presentation to include several childhood photos. Furthermore, I came up with a few personal stories to help reinforce the content.

Although I liked the changes, I couldn't help but feel anxiety. *"What if I am being too vulnerable?"* I thought as the staff grabbed their coffee upon entering the auditorium. *"What if the staff thinks I'm a pushover?"*

When the event began my nerves began to show. I rushed through the welcome and stumbled over new staff introductions. Next, I shared how *"incredible"* the community has been and how *"excited"* I am for this opportunity. Finally, I did the customary *"here is my work experience"* bit.

As I finished reciting my path from high school math teacher to assistant principal to principal to superintendent, I scanned the audience. My new colleagues sat quiet and expressionless. While they weren't heckling or booing me, I was hoping for more enthusiasm in their body language.

Eager to break the tension, I followed the mentor's advice and began describing my upbringing. Flipping through a number of childhood photos, I made fun of my elementary outfits, middle school haircuts, and high school pimples.

Immediately, the pressure in the room diminished. Staff were smiling, laughing, and entertained. The more I let my guard down, the better my message was received. Sensing the momentum, I began telling personal stories, sharing how significant childhood moments impacted my adult life.

I admitted how kids used to call me "Opie" (from *The Andy Griffith Show*) because I was a scrawny redhead with big ears, and how teasing resulted in self-confidence issues. Later, I discussed the night my parents announced they were getting a divorce, and how this bombshell altered our family dynamics. And finally, I described my ongoing battle with anxiety, and how panic attacks riddled my life as an adult.

Eventually, I transitioned back to the "original" presentation, covering everything from my leadership philosophy to long-term goals. And while I wanted to demonstrate that I had the self-assurance to take on the role, I continued to reiterate that I'm still a work in progress.

After the dust settled from the all-day event, I sat down and opened my email. To my surprise, I received more than a dozen positive messages about the presentation. But it wasn't the educational buzzwords or the fresh initiatives they mentioned, it was the *moments of vulnerability* they admired.

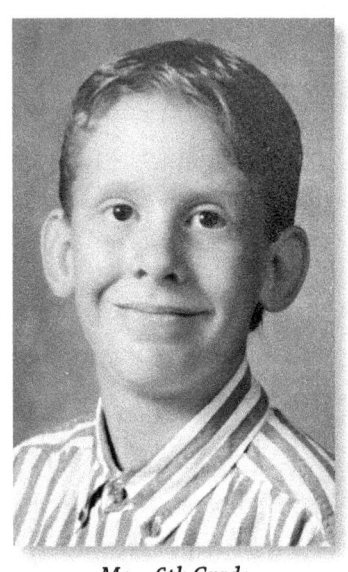

Me—6th Grade

In addition to vulnerability, below are seven concepts for all leaders to consider when preparing their opening-day speech:

Active Participation: Far too many school leaders criticize teachers for using lecture to deliver information to students only to turn around and lecture at employees during their back-to-school speech. Administrators should actively engage faculty in their presentations by encouraging movement, facilitating discussion, and asking for real-time feedback.

Why So Serious? Some school leaders believe every minute with employees must be serious. Certainly, there are times when heavy discussions must be held. However, opening-day speeches are not one of those times. Administrators should create a sense of excitement by infusing music, food, games, and prizes into their back-to-school events.

Our opening-day festivities often involve crowd surfing.

Pay Homage: Upon assuming a new position, there is a natural desire to try and one-up the previous leader. While this is a normal feeling, new administrators must be careful to show respect to the work done prior to their arrival. The opening-day speech is a great time to honor the progress made in previous years.

Establish Core Values: Opening-day speeches are the perfect time for new leaders to share their core values. By discussing the underlying principles that guide their work, leaders not only establish the tone for their leadership, they give employees a preview of how future decisions will be made.

Less is More: Using slides (PowerPoint, Google Slides, etc.) to deliver a message is fairly commonplace. While they are great to reference, slides must support—*not replace*—the message. Most leaders overload their slides with information, when in reality too many words distract the audience. As a general rule, slides should contain no more than 30 words.

Add Pictures: The best public speakers use pictures to tell a story. Not only do photos add variety to a presentation, studies show that visual content is *600 percent* more memorable than written content.[1] While speaking without text can be intimidating, well-placed visuals trigger emotions and promote action far better than words.

Practice Makes Perfect: I'll admit, practicing a speech without spectators feels weird. But once the initial awkwardness passes, rehearsing a speech helps leaders get out of their own head and into the head of the audience. Previously hidden gaps in content and mistakes on slides become blatantly obvious during a verbal run-through.

In *The Gifts of Imperfection*, Brene Brown advises, *"Staying vulnerable is a risk we have to take if we want to experience connection."*[2]

As leaders, we are often taught to keep a distance and project an image of confidence, competence, and authority. However, it is vulnerability that is the source of human connection.

The next time you prepare to address your employees for the first time, consider the following:

Be humble.
Laugh at yourself.
Have fun.
Own your mistakes.
Smile.
Let your guard down.

A little vulnerability goes a long way.

Questions for Discussion:

Reflect: How has your perception of vulnerability in leadership evolved after reading this chapter?

Apply: How might you incorporate elements of vulnerability into your own leadership style or communication approach, especially when addressing a new team for the first time?

Balance: Reflecting on the chapter, how would you strike the balance between projecting confidence and competence while also allowing yourself to be vulnerable in your leadership interactions, particularly in situations like delivering an opening-day speech or addressing a new team?

Optimize: What is one specific practice or technique from the tips provided at the end of the chapter that you can incorporate into your leadership approach to enhance your effectiveness in balancing confidence and vulnerability in your communication and interactions with your team?

Lesson 2

LEAD WITH INTEGRITY

> *"Sportsmanship for me is when a guy walks off the court and you really can't tell whether he won or lost, when he carries himself with pride either way."*
>
> —JIM COURIER

* * *

Pop Quiz: What is the single most important trait for leaders to possess?

Determination? Confidence? Courage? Intelligence?

While those are great guesses, research indicates *integrity*—the quality of being honest and having strong moral principles—is the most essential quality for highly effective leadership.[3]

"So . . . you're saying administrators should stay out of trouble. Isn't that obvious?"

Clearly, school leaders should avoid making newspaper headlines for the wrong reasons. However, we're not talking about egregious acts of incompetence. Instead, we're talking about a leader who is loyal, reliable, and ethical at all times.

I once worked for a leader who was highly talented.

This individual was motivated, intelligent, and charismatic. Armed with a charming personality and an infectious smile, they were the type of person who could walk into a room and immediately command people's attention.

As naturally gifted as this individual was, there was one small problem: *they lacked integrity.*

For example, this person would often fail to deliver on their commitments. Next, this person played "favorites" with employees as opposed to making merit-based decisions. Finally, this person expected staff to work long hours yet—they themselves—were always the last to arrive and the first to leave.

As time passed, employees eventually lost trust in this individual, resulting in them leaving the district. Despite possessing nearly every leadership characteristic, this person was incapable of being highly effective because they lacked *the* most important trait: *integrity.*

It's hard to discuss integrity without mentioning servant leadership.

Servant leadership is a management style where leaders have a primary focus of serving the employees they lead. Whereas traditional leadership is focused on command and control, servant leadership centers around trust and empowerment.

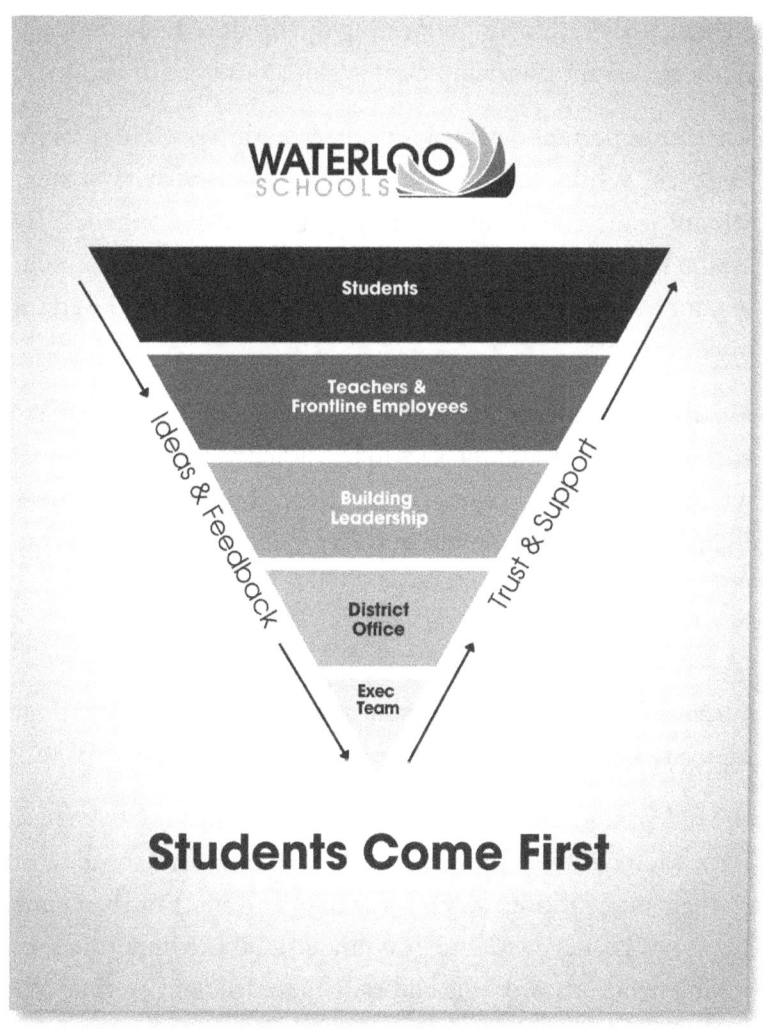

Servant leaders understand the importance of funneling support to frontline employees.

Servant leadership has a trickle-down effect within a school. When administrators focus on meeting the needs of teachers, teachers feel supported and valued. And when teachers' needs are met, they can focus on meeting the needs of their students. In short, servant leadership creates a virtuous cycle of goodwill.

Another important aspect of servant leadership is willingness for feedback. While traditional leaders make decisions in isolation, servant leaders actively seek feedback from the trenches. By asking teachers and other frontline employees for their opinion, servant leaders make decisions that positively impact the entire organization.

Finally, servant leadership creates psychological safety. Leaders with integrity allow employees to be authentic and take chances without fear of retribution. Servant leadership allows employees to innovate, learn from their mistakes, and channel their energy into professional growth.

Curious as to how you can demonstrate integrity in your setting? Here are six ideas to consider:

Active Listening: First and foremost, leaders with integrity know it is their responsibility to listen. Whereas some leaders spend most of their time talking, servant leaders spend most of their time listening. Leaders with integrity understand the importance of asking questions, working endlessly to understand perspectives and provide support.

Follow-through: Few things erode trust more than a leader who fails to follow through on a commitment. Reliable leaders are adamant about being true to their word. Dependable bosses develop systems for keeping track of commitments and let impacted individuals know when action steps are complete.

Model Transparency: Have you worked for a school leader who refuses to share information beyond a select group of individuals? Rather than keep details close to the vest, leaders with integrity understand the importance of sharing information with broader audiences. Furthermore, these leaders understand the importance of explaining the rationale behind decisions.

Loyal to the Absent: Leaders with integrity refuse to say anything about an employee that they wouldn't be willing to say to that employee's face. This can be challenging, especially given how difficult some staff can be! But when leaders are respectful of all employees all the time, they establish an environment where it is unacceptable to disrespect colleagues.

Have Courage: Noble leaders realize it is their responsibility to handle employee issues. Whereas hypocritical bosses condemn poor behavior but refuse to confront frequent offenders, genuine leaders know it is their responsibility to address underperforming employees. Leaders who courageously confront difficult staff immediately earn trust from followers.

Take Ownership: Honorable bosses assume full responsibility for anything that happens under their watch. Whereas some bosses are quick to blame others for mistakes, leaders with integrity understand that significant employee mistakes are typically the result of inadequate training or poor hiring. Furthermore, modest leaders are quick to apologize when errors in judgment are made.

Business tycoon Warren Buffet once said, *"In looking for people to hire, look for three qualities: integrity, intelligence, and energy. And if they don't have the first, the other two will kill you."*

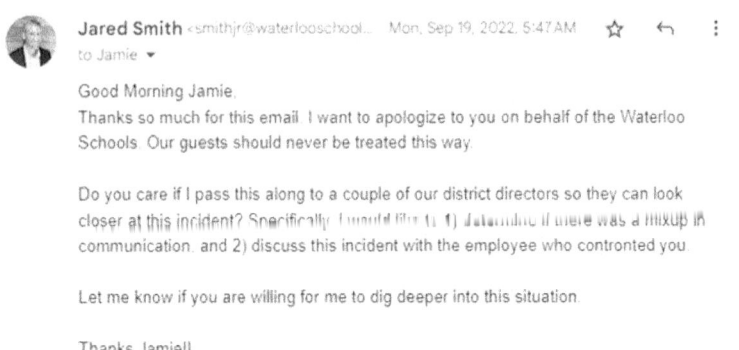

Leaders with integrity assume responsibility for anything that happens within their organization.

School leaders can have all of the enthusiasm, courage, confidence, and wisdom in the world. But if they don't have strong moral principles, the rest doesn't matter.

Integrity is the single most important leadership trait.

Questions for Discussion:

Reflect: How does the concept of integrity in leadership resonate with your personal values and beliefs, and how might reflecting on your own integrity enhance your effectiveness as a leader?

Apply: How might you integrate the principles of integrity discussed in the chapter into your leadership practices when facing challenging situations or making critical decisions within your team or organization?

Balance: How do you navigate the delicate balance between being transparent and sharing information with your team while also maintaining appropriate confidentiality when necessary? Share an example of a situation where you had to strike this balance effectively.

Optimize: Choose one specific aspect of integrity discussed at the end of this chapter, and outline a plan detailing how you will actively incorporate this aspect into your leadership practices.

Lesson 3

Ask Questions

"Great leaders ask more questions than they give answers."

—Kobe Bryant

In 2016, I landed my "dream job." As the head principal of a building with 200 staff and 1,600 kids, I was asked to lead one of the largest high schools in Iowa.

At 34 years old, I was the youngest-ever principal in this building. When I began, I heard words like *"I've been teaching longer than you've been alive"* and *"I'm old enough to be your mom"* from several employees.

Hearing this feedback made me feel good about my professional accomplishments. However, I also wanted to prove that getting the job was no fluke.

To demonstrate my competence, I immediately made changes to our Building Leadership Team (BLT). Without asking for feedback, I told our teacher leaders we were making changes:

who was on the team, the frequency of meetings, the topics of conversation, and our methods for communication.

"We did this in my previous school and it worked really well," I explained via email.

While I didn't think these were big changes, I quickly realized our leaders weren't ready. Almost immediately, I heard grumblings that BLT members were unhappy.

When I asked my secretary what she thought the issues were, she provided some harsh feedback: *"They don't like that you didn't ask their opinion,"* she shared. *"You're just telling them what to do."*

"Ask their opinion?" I rebutted. *"I shouldn't need to 'ask their opinion!' I know what I'm doing."*

This standoff between me and the BLT lasted for months. Despite creating tension with key building leaders, my pride couldn't handle being wrong. *"If I give in now, they won't respect me in the future,"* I worried.

While our team eventually adjusted to my ideas, the damage was already done. I senselessly created adversarial relationships with important individuals—relationships that took months to recover.

It turns out I made this fatal leadership mistake: *I was telling instead of asking.*

"The best leaders are great listeners," said James Kouzes and Barry Posner in *The Leadership Challenge*. "They listen carefully to what other people have to say and how they feel. They ask good questions, *are open to ideas other than their own, and even lose arguments in support of the common good."*

It took more than 10 years in administration to finally understand the importance of listening. But when I did, I noticed three significant changes.

First, I learned that listening improved employee engagement. When I started asking employees to share their opinions, they felt more valued. Not only did employees feel more committed to the work, asking questions created a feeling of mutual respect which led to deeper relationships between me and those individuals.

Don't forget food service employees when it comes to asking for input.

Second, I learned that listening helped me hone my decision-making skills. My younger self didn't think it was necessary to ask employees for advice, because—as the leader—I was supposed to be the smartest person in the room. Once I realized the shortsightedness of my thinking, I discovered that employees had a lot of great ideas . . . many of them better than my own.

Third, I learned that listening made my job easier. Early in my career, when staff came to me with concerns I immediately felt compelled to give them answers. However—once I started asking questions instead of giving answers—I noticed that employees were fully capable of solving problems on their own. This prevented me from assuming the burden of employee issues.

"But shouldn't leaders assume the burden of employee issues?" you may be thinking. *"Isn't that 'servant' leadership?"*

While getting involved in every employee issue sounds noble, in reality bosses do not have the bandwidth to assume this responsibility. Administrators who stubbornly insist that every employee issue runs through them create a massive organizational bottleneck where employees wait days (if not weeks) to be told what to do.

Instead, administrators should help employees work through problems by asking questions and trusting employees to make their own decisions.

The key to being a great listener is knowing which questions to ask. Here are five powerful prompts that can spark productive conversations and strengthen relationships:

"What's going on in your world?" While there are several ways to start a conversation, this prompt is effective for a couple reasons. First, this question ensures that the conversation is focused squarely on the employee. Second, the open-endedness of the inquiry gives subordinates complete control over where the conversation goes next.

"What's keeping you up at night?" Did you know that nearly half of American employees lose sleep at night worrying about work?[4] Not only does this question resonate with employees, it helps skip over surface level issues while focusing on the topics that matter most to employees.

"What barriers are you experiencing?" Whether it be a personality conflict with a coworker, the need for additional training, a lack of financial resources, or a need for clearer expectations, asking employees to name specific barriers gives administrators an opportunity to understand their employees' current reality.

"What are your next steps?" Too often, administrators tell employees what to do as opposed to helping them process challenging situations. This question empowers staff to take ownership of the current problem while also building their capacity for handling future issues.

"What do you need from me?" While some leaders may fear this question will result in an unreasonable request, most employees are good about respecting their supervisor's time and will decline

an offer for assistance. The beauty of this question is that both sides are clear about the leader's next steps.

※ ※ ※

Steve Jobs famously said, *"It doesn't make sense to hire smart people and tell them what to do; we hire smart people so they can tell us what to do."*

Don't make my same rookie mistake:

Stop *telling* employees what to do.
Start *asking* employees what to do.

Questions for Discussion:

Reflect: Reflect on your current leadership style: Do you find yourself more often telling others what to do or asking for their input? How does this approach affect your relationships and the effectiveness of your team?

Apply: Think about an upcoming meeting or project. How might you incorporate the practice of asking questions instead of giving directives to better engage your team and improve outcomes?

Balance: How do you strike the balance between gathering enough input from your team and making a decisive decision as a leader?

Optimize: In what ways could you integrate the questions suggested at the end of the chapter into your leadership practices to foster better communication and engagement with your team?

Lesson 4

NOT KNOWING IS OKAY

*"Show me a guy who's afraid to look bad,
and I'll show you a guy you can beat every time."*

—Lou Brock

Several years ago, a community member approached me at a wrestling meet.

This individual had questions about property taxes and they came to me seeking answers.

As a high school assistant principal, I had a baseline understanding of school finance. But to say I thoroughly understood property taxes would be a stretch.

I quickly realized I did not have an answer to this question. Embarrassed, I proceeded to give my best response, while admitting I needed to do some checking and get back to this person.

I'm sorry," responded the gentleman. *"I figured you would know since you're an administrator."*

Disappointment consumed my emotions upon leaving the event. I took pride in having answers, so not knowing what to tell this curious stakeholder made me feel like an imposter.

※ ※ ※

School leaders are asked dozens of questions throughout the day. Questions can be diverse, ranging from special education law to hot lunch prices to parent visitation rights.

In these situations, leaders often feel pressure to have answers. *"I'm in charge, I should know this"* is a common feeling, leading some administrators to make guesses or give incorrect answers as opposed to admitting *"I don't know."*

But rather than knowing everything, administrators must realize that *not* knowing is okay. The world of education is incredibly complex and nuanced, making it impossible for any one person to know every detail relevant to their position.

In addition to admitting when they don't have an answer, leaders are advised to use a counterintuitive tactic: asking "dumb" questions.

Savvy leaders develop a sixth sense for realizing when basic, underlying questions need to be asked. When bosses bring dumb questions to the surface, two things happen: *clarity* is provided to the topic being discussed and *permission* is given for others to be vulnerable.

Consider the various meetings you attend. Do you believe everyone at the table has a deep understanding of the topics being debated? Often, attendees are limited in their knowledge and are trying to play catch-up while others are talking. But rather than publicly admit their confusion, these individuals avoid embarrassment by nodding their head and going along with the group.

By scanning the room, reading body language, and knowing the strengths of their people, effective leaders pause the discussion when they realize unanswered questions are lurking. This takes confidence and humility, but—when properly applied—results in shared understanding and informed decision-making.

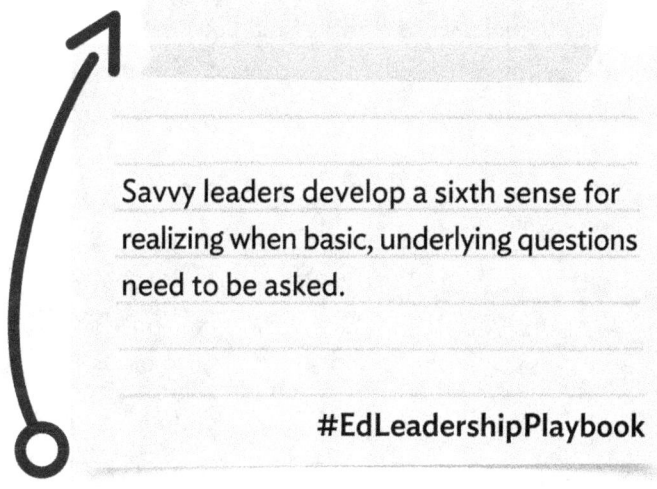

Savvy leaders develop a sixth sense for realizing when basic, underlying questions need to be asked.

#EdLeadershipPlaybook

Being comfortable not knowing also comes in handy with a sneaky group of individuals we'll call "fast-talkers."

Fast-talkers are people who are assertive and articulate. Whether they are an employee, a parent, or a community member, these individuals prey on school leaders, leaders while looking for opportunities to push their agenda forward with little to no resistance.

Salespeople are another example. When you move into a leadership role, suddenly *everyone* wants your business. Yearbook representatives to fundraising marketers to professional speakers—these people appear out of thin air when you become the person in charge.

Some salespeople talk so quickly and are so convincing that it's overwhelming. But rather than pause the conversation to seek clarity, many administrators simply nod their head in agreement.

Do not fall into this trap! As a leader, recognize that it's your responsibility to make sense of things and don't move on until you do. If you're feeling pressured, calmly declare, *"I'm sorry, but you're going to need to slow down so I can understand what you're saying."*

It's a trap!

In addition to admitting when they don't know something, administrators must encourage employees to do the same. The following are seven strategies for creating a workplace where staff feel comfortable speaking up:

Be Intentional: Administrators must constantly remind employees that not knowing is okay and it's important to ask questions. Purposefully inserting phrases into meetings such as *"Does this make sense to everyone?"* and *"This is a safe space for asking questions"* gives employees permission to admit when they have lingering questions, doubts, and concerns.

Lead by Example: Leaders must always be willing to "go first" when it comes to admitting that they don't know something. Administrators who have the courage to say *"Is anyone here besides me confused?"* or *"Can I ask a dumb question?"* show others that it's okay to pause the conversation when underlying context is missing.

Visibility: Being visible is one of the best ways for administrators to create a safe space for asking questions. Sometimes, staff refuse to ask questions in a formal setting, regardless of how safe the environment is. But when administrators proactively visit classrooms and offices, they find that employees are more willing to open up and ask their questions or concerns.

Email Me: Administrators who are constantly on the go get asked several questions throughout the day—many of which they don't have an immediate answer to. In these situations, administrators should ask employees to email their questions. Emails ensure that the employee request is not forgotten, and give administrators time to find an answer.

Set the Tone: When communicating information through email, administrators should remind employees that it's perfectly fine to ask questions. Furthermore, employees should be directed where they can go if they have questions. Adding this one additional statement to important communication creates an atmosphere of support and openness.

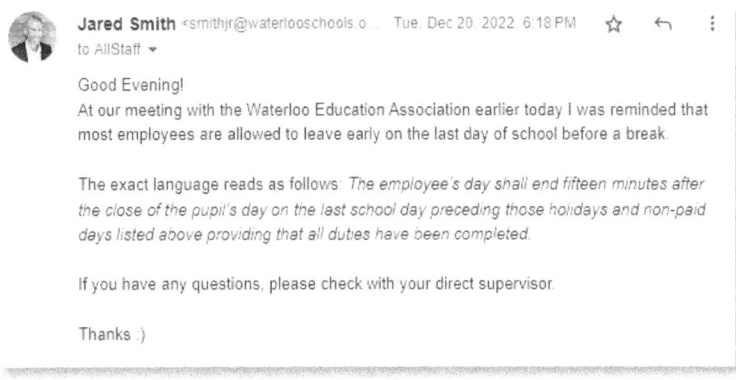

Always let employees know it's okay to ask questions.

Explain: Far too often, administrators take for granted what employees know about school processes. Topics such as school funding, board policy, and building construction are often glossed over and rarely discussed. When administrators give a behind-the-scenes look at district operations, employees feel more connected to the broader organization.

Take the High Road: School administrators should never make employees feel bad for asking a question—*especially* in the presence of others. While some staff are overly inquisitive and some questions might feel random, school leaders should always be tactful in their response to protect the dignity of their employees.

I love helping others.

When someone asks me a question, I want to have an answer.

Rather than feel embarrassed, I now feel comfortable saying, *"I'll be honest—I don't know. But I'll get back to you with an answer."*

Stop thinking you have to have all the answers.
Instead, understand that not knowing is okay.

Questions for Discussion:

Reflect: Reflecting on the experiences and insights shared in this chapter, how comfortable are you with admitting when you don't know something, and how do you typically respond in those moments?

Apply: How might you create an environment in your workplace where both you and your colleagues feel comfortable admitting when you don't know something and are encouraged to ask questions?

Balance: How can you balance the confidence to admit when you don't know something with the need to maintain your credibility and authority as a leader?

Optimize: Which strategy from the end of the chapter will you implement to enhance your practice, and how do you plan to integrate it into your daily routine?

Lesson 5

EMBRACE CRITICISM

"The way I've been brought up to is take critiques and turn them into positives in my game."

—ALEX MORGAN

One trait of effective leadership is the ability to embrace criticism.

Embracing criticism is the willingness to listen to and consider criticism, feedback, or suggestions without becoming defensive or taking it personally. And while it's never easy to hear, effective leaders understand significant professional growth is impossible without the occasional criticism.

Unfortunately, many leaders struggle with this concept. Rather than listen with an open mind, prideful individuals shut down and become defensive upon receiving feedback that is critical in nature. Making matters worse, some leaders hold grudges towards individuals who provide even the slightest of critiques.

Consider the administrators you work for: *Would you feel comfortable sharing feedback that is critical of their performance?*

Sadly, very few school leaders create an environment where others are empowered to share constructive feedback.

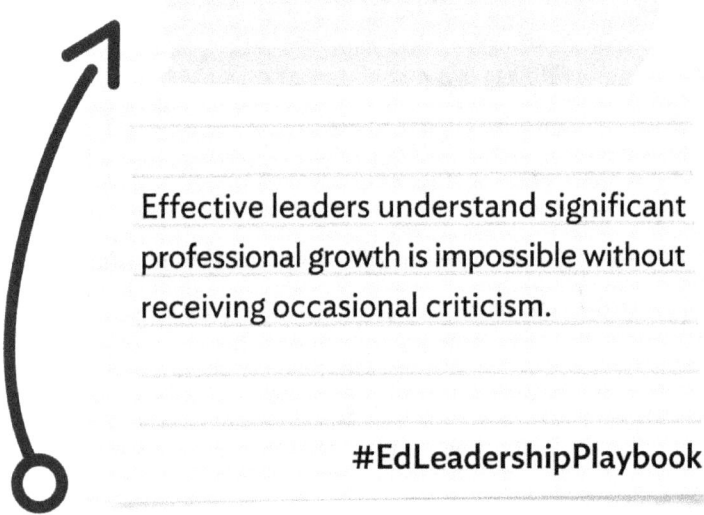

Effective leaders understand significant professional growth is impossible without receiving occasional criticism.

#EdLeadershipPlaybook

***

Toward the end of my first year as a superintendent, I spent several weeks developing a document that would serve as our district's strategic plan.

When the document neared completion, I asked our leadership team for feedback. Despite asking for suggestions, I didn't think anyone would actually take me up on my offer. So imagine my surprise when two instructional coaches asked to discuss the document.

When I met with the employees, they provided several suggestions for improvement. On the outside, I nodded my head and smiled upon hearing their critiques. But on the inside, I was fuming: *"Do they realize how much time I've spent on this? If you think you can do better . . . be my guest!"*

We met for about 30 minutes. With each passing comment, I grew more agitated. Not only was I annoyed with the coaches for thinking they were smarter than me, I was frustrated at myself for seeking feedback in the first place.

When the meeting ended, I thanked the employees for their time and gave them a (fake) smile as they left my office. As they drove away in their cars, I couldn't help but think of the hours that were wasted if I made the changes.

It took a week until I was mentally prepared to revisit the strategic plan. But when I did, I realized the criticism was warranted. My draft was far too wordy and would be difficult for most employees to follow. The instructional coaches were accurate in their assessment that the strategic plan needed to be understood by *all* employees, not just teachers.

I spent several hours revising the document based on our coaches' feedback. And in the end, the document was outstanding. Not only did our strategic plan resonate with stakeholders, the final product was used as a model for other districts around the state.

A few days later, I sent the following email to both employees, thanking them for having the courage to share their constructive feedback:

>
>
> **Smith, Jared** <jsmith@s-tama.k12.ia.us> Thu, Aug 1, 2019, 5:35 AM
> to Seth, Kathy
>
> Hey Kathy! Unfortunately everything has "gone to press"!! I actually pick up the finished products tomorrow!!
>
> I'll see if I can find the final drafts and send them your way :)
>
> I wanted to say THANKS again for the feedback you and Seth gave. What you shared completely changed the complexion of the two documents we finished with. You will notice that both documents ended up being only four pages in the end!! Initially, when you gave me the feedback internally I was dealing with a little bit of defensiveness and a feeling of, "But I put in all that work!!"... But being open-minded to your suggestions got us to a point where I believe we have an end-product that is as good as any I have seen across the state.
>
> Like I said before - the key thing is getting the project right regardless of our feelings. It's not the easiest to do, but when you have good people you can trust the end result will be much higher quality.
>
> So this may sounds like an over-exaggeration but I truly believe much of the end product can be traced back to the two of you having the courage to provide feedback. So THANKS!!!! :)

Another example of willingness to accept criticism happened during the summer of 2020. It was during this time that school leaders were tasked with developing plans for returning to school during the COVID-19 pandemic. These decisions were not easy and were heavily criticized in many communities.

Prior to the start of school, I met with a group of upset parents who did not agree with our school district's plan to begin the year with remote teaching and learning. And based on the intelligence I had received, these parents were livid and out for superintendent blood.

Sure enough, when the meeting began the parents immediately began criticizing a number of our decisions. One by one, each individual rattled off a laundry list of complaints toward the district.

While the comments were fairly general, I couldn't help but take the feedback personally. I badly wanted to blurt, *"Since when did YOU become an expert on leading a school? What if I showed up to YOUR work and began criticizing YOUR decisions?"*

Despite the attacks, I recalled a passage from Dale Carnegie's *How to Win Friends and Influence People* which reads, *"Even the most violent critic will frequently soften and be subdued in the presence of a patient, sympathetic listener."* [5]

With this in mind, I made sure to show genuine interest in each individual who spoke by establishing eye contact, nodding my head, taking notes, and asking clarifying questions.

Eventually, fervent hostility gave way to healthy dialogue. The parents did an admirable job describing how the plan for remote learning would impact families, while also offering feasible solutions. By the end of our conversation, we had gained a mutual understanding and even shared a few laughs.

Later that evening, I received the following message from one of the more outspoken parents: *"Thank you so much for sitting down today and listening to some concerns! I'm definitely feeling better about some things. We are lucky to have you here!"*

This brings us to the concept of being coachable.

Being coachable means an employee is receptive to feedback from supervisors, peers, and colleagues. Furthermore, being coachable means an employee will actively use feedback to improve their workplace performance.

Supervising coachable employees is one of the most rewarding aspects of leadership. Employees who are hungry to improve and open to feedback are easy to manage and a pleasure to work with.

In contrast, supervising uncoachable employees is among the biggest leadership challenges. Employees who are close-minded and resist feedback are difficult to manage and frustrating to work with.

Consider the employees you currently supervise. Can you think of someone who resists coaching? Usually these individuals are easy to identify because of their arrogant personality and toxic behavior.

Unfortunately, those who resist coaching impede their career advancement. One could argue that being coachable is the *single most important trait for internal promotion.* Rarely do uncoachable employees move up the ranks in healthy organizations.

Finally, understand that being coachable does not equate to a lack of confidence. In fact, employees who are open to feedback are typically more self-confident, as they possess the courage to acknowledge areas for growth while actively seeking to better themselves.

Now that we have established the importance of embracing criticism, how can leaders encourage others to share constructive feedback? Here are six ideas to consider:

Solicit Feedback: Whenever possible, leaders must tell employees they are open to constructive criticism. I often remind our staff: *"The only way I can get better is to understand my blind spots."*

Leaders who admit they don't know everything and want critical feedback build trust with followers.

Bite Your Tongue: A fight or flight response is common when we are criticized. But rather than argue, leaders must pay close attention to what is being said. People who get defensive effectively kill any chance of getting feedback from that person in the future. In short, *never criticize the criticism.*

Body Language: Nonverbal communication plays a huge role in how others perceive you as receiving feedback. Resist rolling your eyes, crossing your arms, and averting your gaze as others speak. Instead, use affirmative movements such as maintaining eye contact, nodding your head, and smiling when appropriate.

Express Gratitude: Regardless of how bad it hurts, leaders should show appreciation for feedback. One of my favorite lines to use is: *"I appreciate you having the courage to share your perspective."* Even if I don't necessarily agree with the feedback, I always acknowledge the individual's point of view.

Don't Dwell: In the past, negative feedback would put me in a bad mood for days. I've now rewired my brain to treat feedback as a blessing in disguise. Assuming your job isn't in danger, accurate criticism should be viewed as the *best* feedback you can receive.

Follow-Up: After some time has passed, look for opportunities to tell people how their critical feedback has made a difference. Not only will this build a strong relationship with that individual, you also increase the likelihood of that individual being open to their own constructive feedback.

Let's be real: receiving criticism is never fun.

However—once you get over the momentary sting—criticism can be transformational. Not only will your leadership improve, you can strengthen relationships in the process.

As Kelly Clarkson once said, *"What doesn't kill you makes you stronger."*

Questions for Discussion:

Reflect: Reflect on a recent instance where you received constructive feedback. How would the person who provided that feedback describe your response/reaction?

Apply: Identify a current project or task you are working on. How might you use the principles of embracing constructive feedback to improve your work?

Balance: How can you strike a balance between embracing constructive feedback and not taking it too personally or feeling obligated to use every suggestion?

Optimize: Identify one or two strategies for embracing constructive feedback mentioned at the end of the chapter. How might you use these strategies to enhance your own practice?

Lesson 6

Build Relationships with Staff

> "Players don't care how much you know
> until they know how much you care."
>
> —Pat Summitt

When I began my administrative career, I was required to attend an orientation for new assistant principals.

As part of the two-day training, there was a panel discussion where veteran administrators fielded questions from novice leaders. One topic of conversation was administrator/employee friendships. Specifically, new leaders were wondering what rules to follow when building relationships with employees.

After a few minutes of dialogue, it became clear the experienced administrators were advising newcomers to be cautious in their relationships with employees.

"Be really careful," insisted one mentor.
"Not a good idea," suggested another.
"You'll regret it," said a third.

Toward the end of the conversation, one outspoken administrator issued the following warning: *"Get used to drinking by yourself in your basement."*

While facetious in nature, this statement summarized the overwhelming sentiment of the panel which was that *administrators should keep staff members at a distance.*

As I walked out of the session, I wasn't sure what to believe. Growing up, my parents taught me to be friendly and attentive to everyone. In high school, I learned that leadership is about influencing others. And as a teacher, I was reminded of the importance of relationships.

"Maybe leading adults requires a different approach?" I thought to myself.

A few minutes later, I thought about the leaders I worked under as a teacher. Of the ten or so administrators I worked for, there wasn't one in which I had a strong relationship. Other than your typical formal observation or classroom walk-through, I couldn't recall a single time when a leader went out of their way to engage me in meaningful conversation.

"Maybe these veteran administrators are onto something" I pondered while driving home from the conference.

Taking this advice to heart, I began my administrative career committed to avoiding close relationships with employees. I skirted conversations unrelated to work, rarely asking employees about family members or personal interests. Furthermore, I isolated myself whenever possible, sitting alone at meetings and trainings as opposed to actively engaging with staff.

Everything changed approximately six months later when I received an email from a veteran teacher. This individual was a fantastic educator and highly respected in our building.

The email began, *"I wish you would get to know us."*

She then gave a detailed summary of her life, describing her husband, kids, hobbies, and career path.

She ended the email with: *"Please spend more time getting to know your teachers."*

My heart sank upon reading this email.

She was completely right. By refusing to let my guard down around employees, I was doing the *exact opposite* of what effective leaders should do. While experience told me to behave one way . . . my conscience was telling me otherwise.

From that point forward, I focused on building relationships with employees.

BUILD RELATIONSHIPS WITH STAFF | 43

School leaders should not be afraid to let their guard down with employees.

❖ ❖ ❖

Managerial myth says leaders shouldn't get too close to their employees.

Let's set this myth aside.

Employees who have a friendly relationship with their boss report being more engaged, motivated, happier, and more content than employees who do not feel a similar connection.[6]

"But Jared, I have 100 employees," you may be thinking. "How can I possibly build relationships with everyone?"

While the depth of most workplace relationships depends on proximity and access, steps can be taken to strengthen connections with *all* employees. Here are seven of my best ideas:

Every Interaction Matters: In our district, we believe that every employee matters. Furthermore, we stress that every employee *interaction* matters. Bosses who are serious about building relationships realize there is no such thing as a "trivial" conversation. Instead, they treat each interaction as an opportunity to positively impact an employee's life.

Invest Time: Bosses who are serious about building relationships invest time in their people. *"But I talk to my employees all the time,"* you might be thinking. Unfortunately, hallway chitchat and meeting small talk do little to build strong connections. Leaders must routinely give employees their undivided attention for sustained periods of time.

Social Media: One of the most efficient methods for building relationships with a large number of employees is social media. Social media is where staff share what is most important in their lives. Leaders who take time to like, comment, and—most important— *learn* about their employees, do wonders to strengthen connections.

Email: Another high-leverage opportunity to build relationships with employees is email. *"Email?"* you may be thinking. *"That feels so impersonal."* Whereas most people view email as a necessary evil, savvy leaders use email to build relationships with employees by not only validating feelings, but also by looking for opportunities to show appreciation for the employees they supervise.

Jared Smith <smithjr@waterloos... Tue, Nov 15, 2022, 5:12 AM
to Brian, Stephanie, Andy

Good Morning Brian!
I wanted to take a moment to let you know that your name has come up numerous times in terms of someone who is ROCKING their new job this year.

In the past two weeks I have not only heard how helpful you have been with parents and students. I've also heard you have been a great team player and go above and beyond to help employees. Furthermore, I have been in two separate meetings where I have been told that you have a great presence in the hallways and have been instrumental in getting kids to class while limiting issues between periods.

Finally, I was impressed with the PBIS session you led at the TQ day. You did a great job of sharing your expertise while also being vulnerable in your limited knowledge on how PBIS translates to the secondary level. Your down-to-earth approach was very much appreciated by myself and those I was sitting around.

In short - we are LUCKY to have you back in the Waterloo Schools!!

Have a great Tuesday and a wonderful Thanksgiving :)

Jared R. Smith, Ph.D.
Superintendent
Office Phone: (319) 464-1329

Education Service Center
1516 Washington St. | Waterloo, IA 50702
www.waterlooschools.org

Birthday Emails: One of the most efficient methods for building relationships with dozens (if not hundreds) of employees is by sending birthday emails. Once birthdays have been imported into your electronic calendar, send employees a heartfelt message on their big day. You would not believe how many employees are shocked by these unexpected messages!

Don't Forget Support Staff: Despite making up nearly half of the school workforce, support staff often feel neglected by administration. Leaders must be intentional about visiting the spaces where food service, custodians, bus drivers, and other support staff are located. Simply popping in and saying *"Wow, your team has been crushing it recently—we appreciate everything you do!"* goes a long way toward building rapport with those individuals.

Food: One of the best ways to build inroads with staff is food! On Monday mornings, I hand deliver candy to district office employees. And one Friday a month, I hand deliver donuts to employees in one of the 20 buildings in our district. Not only do staff love a treat to start their day, I also get an opportunity to positively engage with a large number of employees in a short amount of time.

Donut Fridays are one of my favorite traditions!

As I reflect on my first year as an administrator, I'm embarrassed by my thoughts about building relationships with employees.

Don't make my same mistake.

Rather than distance yourself from staff, get to know your employees on a personal level.

Not only will you be a better leader, your school will be better as a result.

Questions for Discussion:

Reflect: Reflecting on the experiences and strategies shared in this chapter, how would you describe the current state of your relationships with your colleagues or staff members?

Apply: In what ways might you integrate the insights on building relationships with staff from this chapter into your daily interactions and leadership approach?

Balance: In your role as a leader, how do you manage the challenge of building rapport with your staff while also maintaining professional boundaries?

Optimize: Which strategy or strategies from the suggestions at the end of the chapter do you plan to adopt to enhance your approach in building relationships with your staff?

Lesson 7

Make Time for People

"I always tell kids, you have two eyes and one mouth. Keep two open and one closed. You never learn anything if you're the one talking."

—Gordie Howe

School leaders are busy.

Walk into any building and leaders can be seen darting through hallways and classrooms to ensure the day runs smoothly. When leaders are on the go, it is easy to have a one-track mind: *Solve one issue and on to the next.*

Unfortunately, leaders who operate with tunnel vision often fail to notice the most vital aspect of their job: *People.*

"How can a leader walk right by a group of people they work with and not even say hello to them?" [7]

When I initially read this in John Maxwell's *The 21 Irrefutable Laws of Leadership*, I didn't believe this issue pertained to me. I was always respectful of employees and certainly didn't pass them without acknowledgment.

However, reading further I realized there was more personal truth than I first believed, *"Don't say 'I've got a lot of work to do today and I really want to get started.' You just walked past your work. Never forget that leadership is about people."*

And then it dawned on me: Although I make time for employees, I always struggle giving employees my full attention. Especially when in the back of my mind *"more important"* work needs to be done.

As an assistant principal, a colleague nicknamed me *"The Red Flash"* due to my red hair and my penchant for dashing around the school putting out fires. While I was a pro at responding to building *"emergencies,"* I was a novice when it came to slowing down and investing time with staff.

As a principal, my nickname did not continue, but what did continue was my bad habit of choosing problems over people. In a large building with hundreds of students and staff, my attention was often focused on addressing *"pressing"* student matters—at the expense of staff relationships.

As a superintendent, one would assume I had finally learned my lesson about workplace priorities. But while initially disciplining myself to spend time with staff, eventually I reverted back to a mindset where completing *"urgent"* office work was more critical than listening to employees.

Old habits die hard.

■ ■ ■

Energy is precious and the brain is wired to conserve it whenever possible. Therefore, it is human nature to follow *The Law of Least Effort*. This principle suggests when deciding between two options, people naturally gravitate toward the choice requiring the least amount of work.

Often, this concept pertains to our personal life. Rather than clean out the garage or go for a bike ride, our tendency is to select easier options such as scrolling through our phones or watching Netflix.

The Law of Least Effort impacts work as well. School leaders have many options for how to spend their time, with varying levels of energy needed to complete each task. For example, when a school leader enters the office, they are faced with two options: Stop to engage with one's secretary, or proceed to their desk to begin work.

While conversation seems like the easier option, the reality is many supervisors choose the latter.

Why is this?

First—let's face it—many bosses are awkward around staff. One survey found 69 percent of managers are uncomfortable speaking with employees.[8] It's one thing to feel uneasy giving bad news or constructive feedback, but this survey indicates a large majority of leaders feel uneasy when forced to converse with staff.

Second, leaders are notorious for becoming obsessed with solving work issues. Have you ever laid awake at night, unable to sleep as you ruminate on a work issue? Fixating on work-related problems makes it difficult for leaders to give their full attention to other matters, and those closest to them often bear the brunt of this behavior.

Let's take a closer look at support staff.

When educators transition into leadership roles, they suddenly find themselves surrounded by a dedicated group of secretaries, clerks, registrars, counselors, student safety personnel, and other administrative professionals.

Often, leaders tend to take these employees for granted. Sure—when we assume a new role—we go above and beyond to get to know our team. However, as the months go by and we settle into our jobs, we aren't as intentional about reinforcing those relationships.

You may be thinking, *"Well this doesn't pertain to me. I have great relationships with my office staff."* Okay then, answer this question: Can you tell me the first names of your coworkers' kids?

If you passed this test, great! You're doing better than most. If you failed this test, what makes you think you can get full effort from someone when you don't know the names of the people dearest to them?

While one question doesn't define your ability to build relationships, it does speak to the notion that leaders must put their "urgent" work aside to focus on their real work—*people*.

* * *

> What makes you think you can get full effort from employees when you don't know the names of the people dearest to them?
>
> #EdLeadershipPlaybook

Beyond learning the names of your colleagues' kids, here are six ideas for strengthening connections with office staff:

Family Quiz: We take getting to know our colleagues to the next level by asking all office staff to give a short presentation on their spouses, kids, and pets. Once this is done, we complete a quiz to see how many names we can remember. Prizes go to the best presentation and quiz score!

Text Thread: Our office staff has an ongoing text thread. Not only does this allow teammates the opportunity to quickly send information to the group, group texts are a fun way to share pictures, keep in touch over breaks, and celebrate accomplishments.

"Get To Know Your Teammates" Quiz: District Office Edition
The winner will receive a GRAND PRIZE!

Name:	Mary Boege
Spouse Name:	
Child Name(s):	
Pet Name(s):	

Name:	Sue Haughey
Spouse Name:	
Child Name(s):	
Pet Name(s):	

Name:	Jon Huebner
Spouse Name:	
Child Name(s):	
Pet Name(s):	

Name	Michelle Kalinay
Spouse Name:	
Child Name(s):	
Pet Name(s):	

Name:	Jessica Poush
Spouse Name:	

People love talking about pets as well!

Shift Attention: Whether it's because they believe they lead more "exciting" lives or they are just poor conversationalists, school leaders talk about themselves way too much. Bosses who intentionally cast the discussion spotlight on staff—*not themselves*—do wonders to strengthen bonds.

Quarterly Meetings: Even though I don't directly supervise all office staff members, I still meet with each individual quarterly. My goal for the meeting is to strengthen my relationship with the employee, while also exploring ways to improve the employee's work experience.

Potlucks: Leaders must prioritize office gatherings, and one of the best ways to do this is through a good old-fashioned potluck. Regularly scheduled potlucks produce positive buzz in the office, while also creating a space for leaders and support staff to engage with one another.

Dress-Up Days: School offices deserve to have fun. Leaders can encourage staff to dress up for special occasions, such as Homecoming, Halloween, the Holidays, and the Super Bowl. Dressing up sparks conversations and strengthens teams while infusing fun and energy into the workplace.

Do you see personal moments with staff as investments or expenditures? Leaders who spend even a few minutes engaging with employees do wonders to instill trust and loyalty.

Sometimes giving 10 minutes to chitchat with a secretary can seem like an eternity. My challenge to you (and me!) is to remember leadership is about *people*.

Next time you make a mad dash to your office to return a phone call or answer an email without acknowledging an employee, remember the following: you just walked past your *real* work.

Questions for Discussion:

Reflect: How often do you find yourself prioritizing urgent tasks over investing time in meaningful interactions with your team or colleagues?

Apply: How might you integrate intentional moments of interaction with your team or colleagues into your daily or weekly schedule to ensure they align with your leadership priorities?

Balance: In what ways might you navigate the balance between prioritizing meaningful interactions with your team and addressing urgent work tasks?

Optimize: Using the ideas from the end of the chapter, describe specific actions or strategies you plan to implement to strengthen relationships and enhance team dynamics.

Lesson 8

Hold Frequent 1:1 Meetings

> *"A life is not important except in the impact it has on other lives."*
>
> —Jackie Robinson

I once worked for a distracted boss.

This boss was constantly working on "important matters" and never had time for employees.

When staff approached this person, they were always told to come back later or schedule an appointment. And when they sat in meetings, this person was always looking at their laptop or checking their phone.

The way this person behaved, we assumed their job was filled with never-ending emergencies and ongoing crises. *"That's why they get paid the big bucks,"* staff would say.

Now that I'm on the other side, I realize this person had us fooled. Certainly, there will be incidents that require an immediate response. However, school leadership is *not* the constant chaos that some bosses lead us to believe.

One of the most valuable gifts leaders can give employees is *undivided attention*. Leaders who invest time in employees foster strong relationships and improve employee engagement. Furthermore, leaders who prioritize listening generate greater buy-in on new ideas and are informed of developing situations before they become bigger issues.

Many administrators say, *"I'm a good listener. I listen to my people all the time."*

But while bosses think they are good listeners, their employees usually feel the opposite. Studies indicate only 12 percent of employees rank their boss as a highly effective listener.[9]

If you think effective listening is a strength of mine, you're wrong. Two of my biggest flaws are a lack of patience and an inability to focus, which makes giving someone my full attention very difficult.

These shortcomings caught up to me as a building principal. Upon finishing my first year, I reflected on the employee relationships I had formed. While I was certainly "friendly" towards employees, I struggled to build deep, meaningful relationships with staff.

Eager to build stronger connections, I asked colleagues for a resource that would allow me to engage staff in deeper conversations. That's when someone suggested I read *Radical Candor* by Kim Scott.

Immediately, Scott's book resonated as she presented several ideas for fostering strong relationships. Specifically, she introduced the idea of regular one-on-one meetings with direct reports: *"1:1s are your must-do meetings, your single best opportunity to listen, really listen, to the people on your team to make sure you understand their perspective on what's working and what's not working."*[10]

I was intrigued by 1:1 meetings. Sure, I was constantly meeting with individual employees. But these meetings functioned as status updates, coaching conversations, and evaluative discussions driven by my agenda. Rarely did I meet with employees . . . *just to listen*.

Eager to give 1:1s a try, I scheduled conversations with our four assistant principals and 10 department chairs. Shortly before the meetings were slated to begin, I started having doubts. *"What will we talk about?"* I worried. *"This is going to be awkward!"*

These fears quickly disappeared when I realized staff had *plenty* to talk about. We discussed everything from resource allocation and curriculum mapping to family happenings and leadership aspirations. The topic of conversation didn't matter. What did matter was staff had their boss's undivided attention.

The feedback was so positive that I scheduled quarterly 1:1s with all 14 individuals. Although they took time, the rapport I built with each leadership team member had a significant impact on relational trust and school culture.

Three years later, I was a superintendent and doing quarterly 1:1 meetings with all 10 of my direct reports when I read *The*

Effective Manager by Mark Horstman. In his book, Horstman promotes the use of 1:1 meetings. However, instead of quarterly meetings, Horstman says that 1:1s should occur weekly.

"Weekly meetings?" I thought upon starting the book. *"That's 10 1:1 meetings a week!! I'll never find time in my schedule."*

Then I came across the following passage:

> *Part of the reason your schedule is so full is because you're not spending enough time with your direct reports. Time spent with your direct reports is the most important time that you will spend at work. If you implement 1:1s you will get more time back in your calendar than you spend having them.*[11]

I floated the idea of weekly 1:1s with our leadership team and was happy to hear they were willing to give this idea a shot. And—almost immediately—weekly meetings paid dividends.

Weekly 1:1s gave me a better pulse on what was happening in the "trenches" of our organization. Being aware of the happenings in each department helped me provide better support to those individuals while also making more informed decisions.

Furthermore, weekly 1:1s gave employees an opportunity to share their biggest challenges. By creating a safe space for brainstorming solutions together, we eliminated small issues before they became bigger problems.

Needless to say, implementing weekly 1:1s was one of the best leadership decisions I've ever made.

Thinking about starting weekly 1:1s in your setting? Here are six ideas to consider:

Surrender Control: Leaders must remember that 1:1s are the *direct report's* meeting. Employees must be empowered to share their most important items while supervisors actively listen and ask clarifying questions. Only after employees are finished should managers share their updates. As a rule of thumb, direct reports should speak at least 75 percent of the time during 1:1 meetings.

Sacred Time: For 1:1s to be successful, supervisors and employees must get into a routine of meeting weekly. When a meeting is canceled, it should be the responsibility of the person canceling to reschedule the meeting. While you may occasionally skip one week, groups should never go two weeks without meeting.

Complete List of 1:1 Meetings for 2021-2022

Name	Brad	Ben	Mark	Sam	Randy	Mary M	Michelle	Steve M	Steve C	Jess
Meeting 1	8/23	9/3	8/26	8/24	8/23	8/26		9/1	8/25	8/25
2	8/30	9/9	9/1	8/31	8/30	9/3		9/9	9/1	9/1
3	9/7	9/16	9/9	9/7	9/7	9/16		9/22	9/9	9/15
4	9/13	9/23	9/23	9/14	9/13	9/30		9/29	9/22	9/22
5	9/20	9/30	9/30	9/22	9/20	10/7		10/6	9/29	9/29
6	9/27	10/7	10/7	9/28	9/27	10/14	10/19	10/13	10/6	10/13
7	10/4	10/14	10/14	10/5	10/4	10/21	11/4	10/20	10/13	10/27
8	10/11	10/21	10/21	10/19	10/18	10/28	11/9	10/27	10/20	11/10
9	10/18	10/28	10/28	10/26	10/26	11/5	11/16	11/3	10/27	11/17
10	10/24	11/5	11/5	11/2	11/1	11/11	11/23	11/10	11/3	12/1
11	11/1	11/11	11/11	11/9	11/8	11/8	11/30	11/17	11/10	12/8
12	11/8	11/18	11/18	11/16	11/15	12/9	12/7	12/1	11/17	12/15
13	11/15	12/2	12/2	11/23	11/22	1/14	12/14	12/8	12/1	1/5
14	11/22	12/9	12/9	11/30	11/29	1/20	1/4	12/15	12/8	1/12
15	11/29	12/16	12/16	12/7	12/6	1/27	1/18	1/5	12/15	1/19
16	12/6	1/11	1/6	12/14	12/13	2/10	1/25	1/12	1/5	2/2

Tracking my 1:1s holds me accountable to meeting with direct reports.

Note Taking: Supervisors are responsible for taking notes during 1:1 meetings. Google Docs are perfect for creating a running list of items discussed that can be transparently shared between both parties. For managers who participate in several 1:1 meetings, written records are crucial for revisiting previous conversations and holding employees accountable.

Running List: Managers and direct reports are both guilty of interrupting each other's daily work with minor issues. Rather than create unnecessary distractions, both individuals should develop a habit of writing their nonurgent items into the Google Doc as a reminder of what to talk about during the weekly meeting.

Timely Feedback: 1:1s are ideal for providing performance feedback. Managers should notice employee actions throughout the week and share those observations during the meeting. While most feedback should be positive in nature, 1:1s are perfect for providing constructive feedback without having to schedule an alarming one-off coaching conversation.

Ongoing Evaluation: The beauty of 1:1 meetings is that they serve as a continuous measure of employee performance. At the end of the year, supervisors should have several pages of notes which serve a comprehensive performance review artifact. Rather than write a new employee evaluation, supervisors save hours of time by printing their meeting notes and using those documents to drive the annual review.

In *How to Win Friends and Influence People* Dale Carnegie suggests, *"Exclusive attention to the person who is speaking to you is very important. Nothing else is so flattering than that."*

Consider the way you treat your employees.

Are you giving employees your full attention?
Or, are you "too busy" with other matters?

Unfortunately, leaders who never listen are eventually surrounded by people who have nothing to say.

Questions for Discussion:

Reflect: Reflect on your recent interactions with others. How often do you give them your undivided attention without distractions?

Apply: Based on the principles discussed in this chapter, what specific steps will you take to ensure you provide your team with your undivided attention during meetings and daily interactions?

Balance: In thinking of your schedule, what might be the ideal frequency and number of 1:1 meetings to effectively support your team?

Optimize: How will you utilize the tips at the end of this chapter to implement more effective 1:1 meetings with your direct reports?

Lesson 9

GIVE ALL EMPLOYEES A VOICE

"Talent wins games, but teamwork wins championships."

—MICHAEL JORDAN

I've had the opportunity to network with countless administrators over the past several years.

During these conversations, I often look for new ideas that can be implemented into my own professional practice.

These discussions have resulted in numerous ideas, such as sending birthday postcards to students, developing a communication protocol for our leadership team, and encouraging a "discipline on wheels" approach for administrators.

However, one novel idea has produced the biggest return on investment: *Rounding Meetings*.

Rounding meetings can be traced back to the health-care field. Rounding is when doctors "make the rounds" to see how patients are doing. These conversations are ideal for patients to discuss their recovery progress and to critique the medical care received. Although simple, physicians have found rounding to be especially helpful because conversations are focused on the *patient*.

The success of rounding in health care has led to extensive implementation in the business world. Rather than visit patients, CEOs, VPs, and managers check in on the status of their employees. During these discussions, supervisors ask how the employee is doing, what issues need to be addressed, and what supports the person needs to be successful. Most important, conversations are focused on the *employee*.

Unfortunately, rounding meetings have been slow to work their way into schools. While many leaders claim *"I check in with my staff all of the time,"* they fail to realize that—at their core—these conversations are dictated by the leader and rarely focus on improving the employee experience.

Whereas the 1:1 meetings discussed in the previous chapter are regular meetings with direct reports, rounding meetings are brief, one-time conversations between leaders and employees for the purpose of building trust and improving the employee experience.

Curious to see what rounding meetings could look like as a superintendent, I committed to completing one 20-minute check-in conversation with every certified employee in our district. When

I told my assistant—Jessica—my plans, she looked at me a little funny: *"You want me to set up meetings . . . with 120 employees?"*

Understand that my calendar is pretty scripted and full of routine meetings, so finding time to schedule so many conversations felt aggressive.

"I know it sounds crazy, but we have the whole year," I assured her. *"Besides, I really want to hear what is going on in our district. Do you think you can come up with a way to schedule these meetings? Pretty please?"*

Jessica playfully shook her head, wrote down a few notes, and assured me she would come up with something.

"I owe you big time!" I told her as she left my office.

My next step was to create a list of questions to ask during each meeting. Scripting questions—as opposed to informal conversation—is preferred for two reasons. First, it documents each conversation. This allows leaders to revisit what was said as opposed to relying solely on memory. Second, it keeps meetings focused. This helps leaders stay efficient with their time when meeting with a large number of employees.

Once meetings were scheduled and questions were written, I was ready to begin. After only a few meetings, I began to realize the incredible impact of rounding meetings. Not only did I get to know each employee on a personal level, I also received great insight about the employee experience.

One of my biggest takeaways from my early rounding meetings was the stress level of our teachers. Because these initial meetings occurred in September and October, I assumed staff would still be in the "honeymoon" period to start the year. So, I was shocked to discover how many employees were already reporting fatigue and burnout.

Scripted questions help rounding meetings stay focused while providing leaders with a running record of their conversations.

Armed with this information, I asked our leadership team to brainstorm solutions. Eventually, we approved a plan to add monthly two-hour early dismissals for teacher planning. The staff welcomed these plans with enthusiasm. Not only did they appreciate additional planning time, employees felt valued because school leaders honored their feedback.

Without rounding meetings, I would have lacked the insight and motivation needed to make this timely decision. Furthermore, the knowledge gained from rounding meetings gave me excellent perspective on numerous topics, helping me know "enough to be dangerous" in conversations with other employees, parents, and community members.

Regardless of your leadership position, rounding meetings are a highly effective practice. Not only do they help build relationships with employees, rounding meetings also help administrators make better decisions.

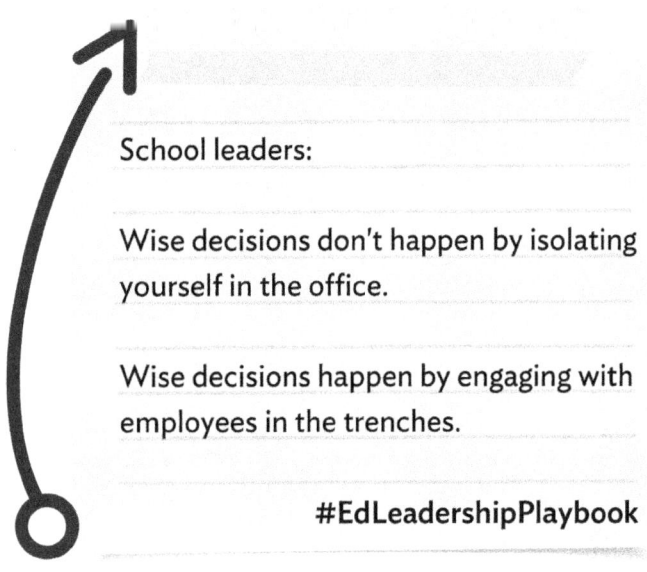

School leaders:

Wise decisions don't happen by isolating yourself in the office.

Wise decisions happen by engaging with employees in the trenches.

#EdLeadershipPlaybook

Thinking about trying rounding meetings in your setting? Here are seven ideas to consider:

No Pressure: Rounding meetings should start light, meaning bosses should encourage employees to share something new or exciting *outside* of work. While some staff may not say much, most employees will find *plenty* to talk about. These stories—whether they are about family, hobbies, or vacations—are a great way to make people feel comfortable and are valuable for future interactions.

Keep Notes: When employees are talking, I type notes directly into the Google Form. While some may worry this disrupts the intimacy of the conversation, I believe notes are essential because they allow me to revisit employee feedback at a later time. Furthermore, having a collection of notes allows me to quickly identify patterns and themes in employee feedback.

Refine Questions: Initially, I asked the following: *"What do you like most about our district?"* Although this question was well-intentioned, I received answers such as *"I like the diversity"* and *"I like the size of the district."* While these were good answers, they did not speak to practices within our control. I found *"What are 1–2 things our district does that you like the most?"* did a much better job of pulling meaningful and actionable feedback.

Build Trust: One of the most important parts of rounding meetings is asking staff to be honest about their workplace experience. In most cases, employees get nervous when sitting face to face with their boss. To put staff at ease, supervisors should use prompts such as, *"You can be honest—it won't hurt my feelings"* and *"This is a safe space"* to promote an environment where employees feel comfortable sharing their true feelings.

Dig Deeper: Once trust has been built, employees may voice frustrations with school leadership, coworkers, or the work environment. When they begin to share their grievances, many staff will pause to gauge their boss's reaction. *"Am I allowed to say this?"* they wonder. Administrators must notice this hesitation and encourage employees to keep sharing, as unearthing these insights is the essence of the rounding meeting.

Follow-Through: As is the case with any meeting, conversation, or survey, bosses must be careful not to waste employees' time. If they don't feel like feedback is being used—*especially after sharing vulnerable feedback*—staff are less likely to trust administration with their time in the future. Bosses must constantly search for opportunities to share how rounding feedback is being used. Team meetings, faculty meetings, and all-staff emails are perfect times for bosses to attribute building decisions to employee feedback.

Positive Feedback: The *"Tell me about one or two people who have been especially helpful I can compliment on your behalf"* question is my favorite part of the rounding process. After the meeting, I copy the positive feedback and paste it into an email that is shared with both the person who was selected and the person who gave the feedback. Quite often, I receive replies such as, *"this made my day"* and *"you made me tear up."* Talk about powerful!

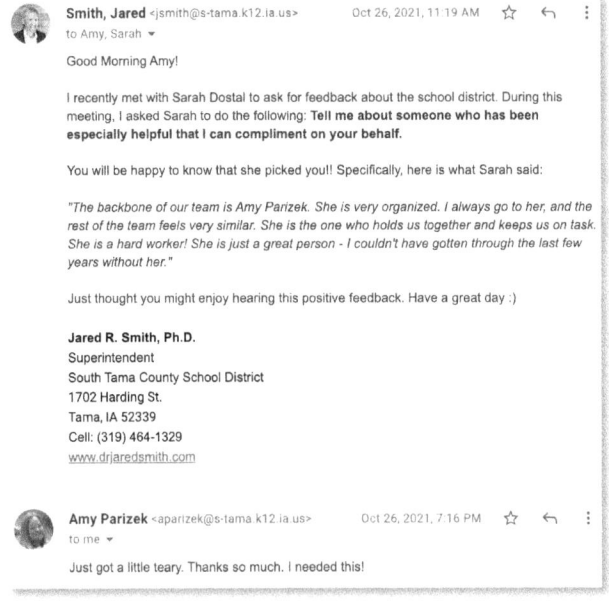

After a rounding meeting with a middle school teacher, I received the following feedback:

> *You have made it feel like you listen to all the teachers. You listen to what we say and you make the best judgment. You don't just sit in the office and make decisions. I've worked in four other districts and haven't seen this before. You actually listen and then make decisions—that's amazing.*

Consider the decisions you make in your own setting.

Are you making guesses based on gut feelings?
Or, do you have evidence based on employee feedback?

Questions for Discussion:

Reflect: In what ways do you currently ensure you hear and consider the perspectives of all employees in your organization when making decisions?

Apply: How might you modify your current approach to decision-making to actively incorporate the perspectives of all employees, based on the insights shared in this chapter?

Balance: Given that you cannot accommodate every perspective, how will you decide which employee input to prioritize and act upon in your decision-making process?

Optimize: How might you integrate the strategies for effective rounding meetings outlined at the end of this chapter into your own leadership practice?

Lesson 10

BE VISIBLE

"Every kid around the world who plays soccer wants to be Pele. I have a great responsibility to show them not just how to be like a soccer player, but how to be like a man."

—Pele

In *Search for Excellence,* Tom Peters and Robert Waterman chronicle a number of successful Fortune 500 companies, seeking common themes across thriving businesses.

One pattern they noticed was that many prosperous companies had supervisors who left their offices to walk around the workplace to engage with employees and observe business operations.

This leadership style was coined *Management by Wandering Around* (MBWA). Despite the name implying an aimless stroll around the office, MBWA is actually a deliberate strategy for leaders to visit their organizational trenches. By observing frontline employees in their element, managers can make more-informed decisions about their company.

Why answer emails from the office ... when you can answer them while listening to a read aloud?

MBWA isn't just beneficial for business leaders; school administrators should also recognize its effectiveness. Rather than governing solely from their office, school leaders should prioritize visiting classrooms and other learning spaces to understand the lived experience of students and staff.

Most important, firsthand perspective is critical for decision-making. Instead of forming opinions based on subjective hearsay and unsubstantiated rumors, leaders who actively engage in the school environment can use personal observations to inform and justify critical decisions.

* * *

Common belief holds that the higher you climb in administration, the more disconnected you become from student learning and the day-to-day operations of a school. Having served as an assistant principal, principal, and superintendent, I've found truth in this sentiment.

As an assistant principal, my days were immersed in the school's daily workings. I handled discipline, assisted teachers, supervised lunches, visited classrooms, and ensured the building ran smoothly. This constant interaction with students and teachers gave me firsthand knowledge of the learning environment.

Transitioning to the role of principal, my responsibilities shifted. While still overseeing the building, I delegated more management tasks related to student discipline and building supervision. As a result, there were times when I missed valuable opportunities to gauge the school's pulse by engaging directly with students and staff.

Now, as a superintendent, I operate from a 30,000-foot view. While this perspective is crucial for vision casting and resource alignment, it leaves me relatively detached from the staff and student experience. My office isn't even on-site—I have to drive off-campus to catch a glimpse of students!

Yet, there are ways to bridge this gap. One effective method is to embrace the MBWA mindset. Administrators who venture beyond their offices into learning spaces—classrooms, hallways, cafeterias, teachers' lounges—discover a wealth of insights. By adopting a servant leadership mentality, they gain a deeper understanding of their school's current reality.

Building	Visit 1	Visit 2	Visit 3	Visit 4	Visit 5	Visit 6	Visit 7	Visit 8	Visit 9	Visit 10	Visit 11	Visit 12
Becker	9/19/22	9/29/22	10/7/22	11/7/22	12/20/22	2/7/23	2/7/23	4/25/23				
Cunningham	8/24/22	10/13/22	12/15/22	1/5/23	1/25/23	4/14/23	5/10/23					
Highland	8/23/22	9/7/22	12/14/22	1/11/23	1/25/23	2/6/23	4/27/23	5/25/23				
Irving	5/18/22	10/12/22	10/20/22	11/2/22	11/28/22	12/8/22	4/14/23	5/2/23				
Kingsley	8/23/22	9/8/22	10/11/22	10/28/22	1/23/23	1/25/23	4/28/23					
Kittrell	8/25/22	10/25/22	12/14/22	12/20/22	1/31/23	4/19/23	4/21/23	5/23/23				
Lincoln	8/23/22	9/26/22	10/6/22	10/31/22	2/7/23	3/21/23	4/25/23	5/16/23				
Lou Henry	9/1/22	10/28/22	12/14/22	2/9/23	3/28/23	4/11/23	5/18/23					
Lowell	8/23/22	9/15/22	11/2/22	1/17/23	2/26/23	2/28/23	4/19/23	5/23/23				
Orange	8/23/22	9/8/22	10/19/22	12/5/22	12/20/22	1/6/23	3/28/23	4/19/23	5/23/23			
Poyner	8/24/22	10/7/22	12/15/22	1/10/23	1/24/23	1/30/23	3/20/23	5/10/23				
Bunger	8/24/22	10/13/22	10/31/22	11/21/22	1/24/23	3/28/23	5/16/23					
Carver	9/20/22	10/20/22	12/8/22	12/20/22	1/6/23	4/14/23	4/25/23	5/11/23				
Central	3/25/22	9/15/22	10/26/22	10/31/22	1/4/23	1/5/23	1/12/23	2/8/23	3/20/23	4/20/23		
Hoover	9/2/22	9/9/22	9/23/22	10/25/22	12/9/22	12/20/22	2/9/23	4/11/23	4/25/23			
East	8/25/22	8/31/22	9/15/22	9/30/22	10/6/22	10/21/22	11/8/22	11/16/22	12/20/22	1/23/23	2/23/23	5/10/23
Expo	9/29/22	10/31/22	12/8/22	12/14/22	12/20/22	3/28/23	4/25/23	5/24/23				
West	8/25/22	9/16/22	9/21/22	9/23/22	10/3/22	10/13/22	12/8/22	12/20/22	1/23/23	3/10/23	3/31/23	5/16/23
WCC	9/9/22	9/19/22	10/25/22	12/14/22	1/5/23	1/12/23	2/8/23	3/28/23	4/20/23	5/11/23		

The spreadsheet holds me accountable for visiting all 19 of our buildings.

One of the biggest barriers to MBWA is the perception of being too busy. *"I'd love to get out of the office,"* these leaders say. *"But I have too much work to do."*

While there are legitimate moments of busyness, some bosses default to *"I'm too busy"* without much consideration. The reality is that a substantial portion of a school leader's work occurs behind a laptop screen. Whether they're responding to emails, analyzing data, or crafting communications, many administrators spend their days tethered to their computers.

However, here's a practical solution: Why not kill two birds with one stone? Instead of working in isolation, leaders can take their laptops into shared spaces like the library, cafeteria, commons, and classrooms. Not only can they complete tasks, but they can also gain insights about their school and earn "visibility points" along the way.

Despite seeming like a reasonable compromise, some leaders resist. Let's address seven common excuses and provide appropriate rebuttals:

"My work is confidential!" Many administrators are concerned that others could stumble upon classified information. Surely, you'll want to refrain from drafting that employee termination letter in the middle of a crowded cafeteria. However, leaders who are mindful of the work they complete in public settings experience few issues.

"I'll be less productive!" Leaders often overestimate their productivity levels when working in the office. Between phone calls, impromptu meetings, and other interruptions, finding a block of time to do anything meaningful is difficult. Ironically, many bosses who bring their work with them realize they are *more* productive with their time.

"I have discipline to do!" Rather than summoning students to the office, administrators should bring their office to students. When I was a building administrator, I would deliberately visit classrooms of students who needed minor behavior consequences. This allowed me to complete a classroom walk-through, while also pulling individual students into the hallway for private disciplinary conversations.

"I'll distract the students!" Some leaders think completing work in a classroom or library will create a distraction for students. I have found the opposite to be true—students are actually on better behavior when an administrator is present. Furthermore, this approach helps administrators get to know their students better.

"I'll distract the teacher!" Some leaders are concerned that they will make teachers and other school employees anxious by unexpectedly visiting their space. To prevent this from happening, school leaders should proactively communicate their plans to regularly visit classrooms and other learning spaces.

"I've got too many (kids/employees/buildings)!" Some large-school principals and superintendents argue that their job is *"too big"* or *"too important"* to get out of the office. Baloney! Whether they manage 300 students or 30,000 students, school leaders must find time to witness teaching and learning. Whenever a meeting is canceled at the last minute, use this gift of time to visit classrooms.

"I'll feel weird!" The first time you work on your laptop in the library or lunchroom, you might feel awkward. *Get over it.* Once you become a regular at working in these spaces, others will get used to—and appreciate—your presence. As with any new habit, getting into a routine helps eliminate most feelings of discomfort.

※ ※ ※

School leaders who embrace a Management by Wandering Around mentality give themselves an opportunity to understand the current reality of staff and students. This firsthand perspective provides administrators with the insight needed to make decisions that accurately reflect organizational needs.

Let's stop with the "*I'm too busy*" excuses and start visiting spaces where the *real* work is being done.

Questions for Discussion:

Reflect: How visible are you within your role, and how might your presence (or absence) impact your understanding of your team's day-to-day experiences?

Apply: How might you integrate Management by Wandering Around into your weekly schedule, and what methods will you use to ensure that you gain valuable insights from your observations and interactions?

Balance: How might you effectively balance the need to be visible and engaged through Management by Wandering Around, while also ensuring that your administrative tasks are completed efficiently?

Optimize: What common excuse noted at the end of the chapter do you find yourself using to avoid practicing Management by Wandering Around, and how can you apply the suggested rebuttal to overcome this excuse and improve your leadership visibility?

Lesson 11

LEVERAGE SOCIAL MEDIA

"People want to be on a team. They want to be part of something bigger than themselves."

—MIKE KRZYZEWSKI

■ ■ ■

For the longest time, school leaders have been advised to avoid being Facebook friends with employees.

"You don't want to get too close to your staff," veteran leaders warned.

For much of my professional life, I followed this advice. When employees sent friend requests, I ignored their advances. Careful not to hurt feelings, I never deleted requests . . . I simply let them sit idle until I left the district. Only after leaving would I accept the dozens of pending friend requests.

A few years ago I decided to use a different approach. Rather than disregard the invitations, I began accepting friend requests from employees. *"Let's see how this goes"* I thought upon accepting my first friend request from a current employee.

At first, only a few staff members added me. But when others noticed I was accepting friend requests, the floodgates opened. Several years later, I am Facebook friends with a significant number of current and former staff.

Whereas I was initially hesitant to change my philosophy, I now believe accepting employee friend requests—and engaging with those individuals online—is my best "secret weapon" for building workplace relationships.

Belgian psychotherapist Esther Perel once said, *"Always take the time to acknowledge people. If you show interest in them, they will be interested in you."*[12]

For bosses who want to acknowledge and show interest in employees, few places are more efficient than social media. While in-person conversations still rule for building meaningful relationships, leaders cannot underestimate the power of social networking.

Social media—Facebook in particular—is where staff share what is most important in their lives. Whether they post pictures of a new grandchild, a wedding engagement, or a family vacation, when something important happens in their lives, staff broadcast the news on social media.

When you have hundreds of employees—like many school leaders do—it can be hard to keep tabs on the latest news. And while leaders don't need to know *everything* that goes on, social media provides quick snapshots of employee milestone moments.

What is particularly advantageous about Facebook friendships is that leaders have two distinct opportunities to make employees feel special. The first opportunity is when the leader initially scrolls through their feed and notices an employee post. When a leader "likes" the post and leaves a positive comment, this reinforces a people-first leadership approach.

"Wow, my boss commented on my post," employees think upon receiving notification. *"That really means a lot!"*

The second opportunity to make the employee feel special happens later when the leader crosses paths with the individual at work. Rather than engage in the classic *"Good morning!"* or *"How are you?"* small talk, the boss can focus attention on the employee by saying *"Your new puppy is so cute!"* or *"How did your 5K race go?"*

Another powerful aspect of Facebook friendships is that they help to eliminate traditional school "hierarchies." In many school settings, support staff feel overlooked and underappreciated. Some school leaders don't even know the names of these employees!

Administrators who engage with support staff on social media do wonders to build relationships with these individuals. In a time when quality paraeducators, custodians, bus drivers, secretaries, and food-service personnel are hard to find, leaders should view Facebook as an opportunity to invest in those employees while also increasing the likelihood that they stick around.

> "Bosses shouldn't be Facebook friends with employees."
>
> Baloney.
>
> Facebook is a gold mine for discovering what is most important in the lives of employees.
>
> #EdLeadershipPlaybook

* * *

"But I don't do social media," some readers may be thinking. *"It's a waste of time."*

I totally get it. Studies have found a strong link between heavy social media use and mental health issues such as anxiety and depression. Furthermore, the addictive nature of social media drains precious brainpower and robs us of time that could be spent on productive activities.

However, school leaders must understand the current landscape. While platforms may change, social media shows no signs of slowing down. With more and more adults using social media, Facebook remains a key space for employee interaction. And while not every leader values these platforms, most employees do.

Leaders who say they *"don't do Facebook,"* miss valuable opportunities to connect with staff. Alternately, leaders who are open to the idea discover that social media provides untapped leverage for building relationships and enhancing workplace culture.

* * *

Thinking about taking this advice and accepting employee friend requests? Here are six tips to remember:

Be Careful: It goes without saying that school leaders must be cautious about what they post. Social media blunders are one of the quickest ways for school leaders to get into trouble. In today's society, far more leaders are fired as a result of careless social media posts than they are low test scores.

Don't Play Favorites: Leaders must remember that some employees will attempt to read between the lines and dissect certain communications. School leaders must remain consistent in how they interact with employees online to avoid giving the impression they favor certain staff.

One-Way Street: While some may disagree, I am not a fan of bosses initiating friend requests. Not every employee wants to be chummy with their boss, which is perfectly fine. Rather than put employees in an awkward situation, bosses should sit back and let staff members initiate friend requests.

Time Commitment: Adopting this professional practice shouldn't take much time. Most school leaders are already on Facebook, and dropping a like or leaving a comment takes only a few seconds. Five to ten minutes every couple days is all that is needed for this practice to be impactful.

Return the Favor: School leaders who engage with employees on social media often notice that those individuals will reciprocate the support. Not only does it feel good when staff like your personal posts, school leaders typically find that employees with whom they have strong online relationships come to their defense when community members question school-related decisions.

Public Culture: Given that Facebook comments are visible to the public, leaders should treat each post as an opportunity to positively impact the broader school community. Leaders who are genuinely thoughtful, enthusiastic, and caring create an online presence that is infectious to others.

■ ■ ■

Traditionalists warn that school leaders should avoid social media interactions with employees.

It's time to rethink this approach.

School leaders who approach social media with an open mind take relationship building to a whole new level.

Questions for Discussion:

Reflect: Reflect on your current practices regarding social media and professional relationships. How do you currently engage with your staff on social media platforms like Facebook?

Apply: Consider the strategies outlined in this chapter. How could you adapt these strategies to effectively leverage social media in your own professional context?

Balance: In what ways might you consider balancing the benefits and challenges of social media engagement with employees to enhance communication and relationships within your team?

Optimize: Based on the tips provided at the end of the chapter, which one or two strategies would you consider implementing or adjusting to enhance your approach to leveraging social media?

Lesson 12

Utilize Effective Communication

"Being a successful driver is not just about individual performance, it's about teamwork and communication."

—Dale Earnhardt Jr.

※ ※ ※

What essential quality do all great leaders possess? *Effective communication.*

Consider the leaders you have worked for.

Some leaders excel at communication. These leaders articulate a clear vision, ensuring every team member understands their roles and responsibilities. These leaders foster an environment of transparency and open dialogue, which motivates employees while cultivating trust and collaboration.

In contrast, some leaders struggle with communication. These leaders' messages are disjointed and vague, leaving staff uncertain about objectives and responsibilities. These leaders unknowingly create an atmosphere of confusion and disengagement, where team members feel undervalued and disconnected.

While some leaders can hide their communication shortcomings, over the long run no leader can be highly effective without strong communication skills.

To be highly effective in today's schools, leaders must operate with transparency.

Transparency involves giving staff, parents, and the broader community a behind-the-scenes look at the day-to-day operations of the school. Whether it's performance data, meeting notes, survey results, or email exchanges, effective leaders seek opportunities to share their work with others.

Leaders who provide an unfiltered view of the inner workings of their school build trust with employees, parents, and community members. When provided with access to information and context behind decisions, stakeholders are less susceptible to believing destructive hearsay and rumors that harm many schools.

If transparency is so advantageous, why do leaders struggle to embrace this approach?

First, most leaders are trained to keep information close to the vest. For years, administrators have been warned about oversharing. *"People don't need to know that!"* others caution. And while social media has completely changed the speed at which information is shared, many leaders still operate with this traditional mindset.

Next, many leaders fear the repercussions of sharing "confidential" information. *"You're going to get sued!"* others warn. Certainly, some student and employee information is sensitive and cannot be shared. However, most information in today's schools falls under the Freedom of Information Act, meaning that the information leaders attempt to withhold is actually a matter of public record.

Finally, control plays a significant role in leaders' reluctance to embrace transparency. *"You're going to lose your authority!"* others argue. Information is power, and many leaders resort to extreme measures to keep that power. Leaders who reject transparency often believe that their power is lessened when subordinates have access to the same information.

To overcome these challenges, leaders must recognize that transparency is not a threat, but an opportunity to strengthen their school community. Administrators who brush aside traditional thinking and embrace a transparent mindset create an environment of trust while also enhancing their own credibility.

Effective communication cannot be discussed without revisiting social media.

In today's hypertransparent world, information is readily accessible and community members are quick to share new on social media. When news happens within our schools, it's only a matter of time until students, staff, and parents "break" the news on their favorite platform.

Today's school leaders must have a strategy to control their school's narrative. Whether they do this on their own—or they have a team helping them—school leaders must actively engage with community members through social media platforms.

Having an effective social media presence allows leaders to share accurate information, provide timely updates, and address misinformation before it spirals out of control. This proactive approach ensures that the school's perspective is heard and understood, rather than allowing rumors and speculations to dominate the conversation.

Unfortunately, some school leaders minimize the impact of social media. While an incident could be common knowledge in the community, some school leaders prefer to remain tight-lipped and act as if nothing happened. And while some school leaders may hesitate to share details for fear of legal repercussions, best practice in today's world suggests a shift toward proactive communication.

Always remember: *When something goes wrong in your school, someone is going to tell your story.* Embracing proactive communication not only allows schools to control the narrative, but also builds trust and helps manage the situation more effectively.

In addition to transparency and controlling the narrative, here are seven more characteristics of effective communication to consider:

Awareness: Administrators must tailor their communication to meet the specific needs of different stakeholder groups, considering their unique perspectives and preferences and customizing their messages. While tailoring messages to meet the individual needs of students, staff, parents, and community members may take more time, it is crucial for effective communication.

Clarity: Clarity is crucial in effective communication. Administrators should avoid using jargon or complex language, and explain any acronyms that might be unfamiliar to their audience. By simplifying their messages, they can ensure that information is accessible to everyone, regardless of their comprehension level.

Diversify: School leaders must use a diverse set of communication channels to ensure messages are delivered to the intended audience. By learning how to mix email, newsletters, social media, phone calls, texting, and face-to-face meetings, administrators can cater to the preferences of various stakeholders.

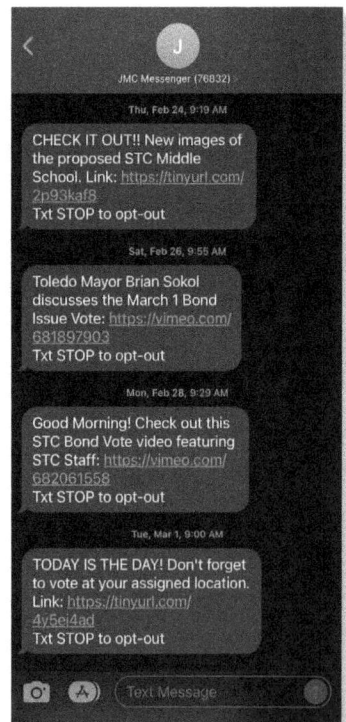

Text Messaging: Text messaging has become so important, it needs its own section. Texts are a critical tool for schools as they offer quick, direct, and efficient communication. *Everyone* has a cell phone, and texting is more effective than emails and phone calls when conveying essential information, such as emergency alerts, event reminders, and weather updates.

Support Staff: Leaders often share information with teachers while leaving support staff out of the loop. It's as if paras, custodians, bus drivers, secretaries, and food service staff are not "worthy" of receiving messages. In reality, effective communication should extend to everyone in the school community, recognizing that *all employees* play a significant role in the school's success.

Feedback: Requesting feedback on the impact of a school's communication is paramount. By actively seeking input, schools can identify areas for improvement, address concerns, and strengthen the overall communication process. Using a feedback-driven approach not only enhances transparency, but it also cultivates a sense of community.

Ownership: Communication is the responsibility of the district, not the community. School leaders like to blame parents when they don't get a message. *"I sent a letter home. I don't know why they didn't show up,"* we complain when a small percentage of families attend an event. Rather than blame the audience, administrators must take ownership of failed attempts and constantly refine their communication methods.

In *Leaders Eat Last*, Simon Sinek highlights the crucial role of communication, advocating that *"effective leaders prioritize open and honest communication"* to build high-performing teams.[13]

Sinek's insights underscore the notion that leadership is about building meaningful connections through communication.

Successful leaders who prioritize effective communication will be rewarded with motivated, high-performing teams that thrive in an environment of shared purpose.

Questions for Discussion:

Reflect: How would your team describe your current communication style?

Apply: What adjustments could you make to enhance trust, alignment, and engagement within your team?

Balance: How do you determine the appropriate balance between radical transparency and information overload when communicating with your team, ensuring openness while maintaining clarity and focus?

Optimize: Drawing from the communication strategies highlighted at the end of the chapter, how might you refine your communication skills to promote transparency and build trust within your organization?

Lesson 13

COLLABORATIVE DECISION-MAKING

"Gettin' good players is easy. Gettin' 'em to play together is the hard part."

—Casey Stengel

* * *

"You don't want too many cooks in the kitchen!"

This phrase is used to suggest when too many people work on the same project, the quality of the final product suffers as a result.

As I moved up the leadership chain, other leaders used this phrase to justify why they made decisions in isolation or with a small inner circle. Assuming these people knew what they were doing, I adopted this mental model to lead several building initiatives.

From grading policies to the student handbook, MTSS processes, and scheduling changes, I believed less staff input was better.

I believed having a small group of individuals at the table would allow us to make the best decision. Furthermore, I figured shutting out the voices of other staff—some of whom would bring conflicting opinions—would save time and energy.

I now realize this approach was ill-advised.

Because they were not involved in the process, staff felt little commitment to decisions that were made. And when marching orders hit snags in the road, frontline employees felt little motivation to actively search for solutions.

"No one asked me," staff would explain. "I could have told you that wouldn't work."

* * *

In *Multipliers*, Liz Wiseman shares the following:

> *When leaders play the role of decision maker, they carry the burden of making the right decision and carrying it through to completion. This can be a heavy burden. But when the leader engages a team in making a decision, they distribute this load to the team. Having worked through the issues, the team will put their full weight behind a decision.*[14]

When you make decisions, where does the burden fall?

Bosses who make decisions alone or with a small inner circle play a risky game. When decisions are correct, leaders come out looking pretty smart. But when decisions are wrong, leaders assume the full burden of the decision. Not only do people question the decision, employees lose trust in the leader's ability to make decisions moving forward.

Rather than make decisions in isolation, leaders must include others in the process. Administrators who actively seek other's opinions generate a comprehensive perspective of the problem, leading to better decision-making. Furthermore, staff who are asked for input are far more likely to support the plan when things get difficult.

"I don't need to worry about this," you may be thinking. *"I always include others in decisions."*

While many bosses believe they promote a culture of collaborative decision-making, research proves otherwise. Studies indicate that 80 percent of leaders believe they actively seek employee input on decisions, whereas only 10 percent of employees believe they are "fully empowered" to help make critical decisions.[15]

If your school or district were surveyed, would this same disconnect occur?

Another important thing to understand is that today's employees want to be a part of the decision-making process. According to *Forbes* Magazine, younger workers *"expect their views to be noticed and acted upon"* at work.[16] And rather than blindly follow directives—as was the case in previous generations—modern employees want to understand why decisions are made.

"I'm sick of younger employees being 'unhappy' at work," some leaders complain. *"They need to stop whining and understand that life doesn't always revolve around them."*

While this sounds reasonable, administrators must understand that the balance of workplace power has shifted. Thanks to a historic imbalance of supply and demand, employees now hold unprecedented leverage on employers, meaning educators will leave for another district when they feel their voice is being ignored.

Looking to improve collaborative decision-making but not sure where to start? Here are seven more ideas to consider:

Explain the Process: When making a complex decision, leaders must tell staff how the decision will be made *before* the process begins. Who will be involved? How is feedback gathered? How long will the decision take? Bosses who invest time to explain the process encounter far fewer issues when a decision is made.

Ask For Feedback: For each decision, leaders must determine *"Who will be impacted by this decision?"* While not every staff member will be able to weigh-in on decisions, leaders must consult with those who are closest to the issue. Don't have the time to meet with several individuals? Online surveys, collaborative documents (e.g., Google Docs), and email help with efficiency.

Leverage Feedback: Have you ever worked for a leader who asked for feedback, but then never explained how the feedback was used? Bosses must get in the habit of reporting how employee feedback drives decisions. This practice is especially powerful when feedback aligns with the decision being made.

All Means All: When decisions are made in a group setting, it is important that *all* voices are heard. Too often, teams will look at the person in the room with the most influence (or the loudest voice) and follow their lead. Leaders must create an environment where all staff are encouraged to voice their honest opinions, even if those opinions differ from the group.

Breaking Ties: When feedback reveals a clear winner, leaders would be wise to make the decision that mirrors the feedback. But what happens when there is no clear solution? This is when leaders must fulfill one of their most important responsibilities: *breaking ties*. Again, leaders who explain this process ahead of time eliminate unnecessary split-decision drama.

Divergent Opinions: What if the group shares a collective opinion that differs from the leader? In most cases, leaders would be wise to yield to the group. While there will be moments when leaders must go against the grain, these instances should be rare. Leaders who adopt a "disagree and commit" philosophy earn the trust and respect of colleagues.

Communicate the Decision: Once a decision is made, leaders must articulate the decision to the broader audience. If the decision was controversial, leaders are advised to explain how the decision was made. In terms of communicating the decision, face-to-face (opportunities for employee questions) and email (clear documentation of the decision) both offer advantages. In a perfect world, leaders explain the decision in person and then follow up with a detailed email.

* * *

I'll admit: I used to *hate* inviting cooks into the kitchen. Not only does asking others for feedback make the decision-making process longer, it increases the likelihood that my idea won't be chosen.

However, I now realize those drawbacks are nothing compared to dealing with the aftermath of a bad decision.

School leaders must eliminate *"You don't want too many cooks in the kitchen"* from their vocabulary. Instead, actively seek input from individuals who will be impacted by the change to ensure their opinions are heard before a decision is made.

Questions for Discussion:

Reflect: Consider a recent decision you made. To what extent did you actively seek and incorporate input from others?

Apply: How might you apply the concepts discussed at the end of the chapter to enhance collaborative decision-making in your own practice?

Balance: In what ways might you strike a balance between ensuring all relevant voices are heard in the decision-making process and avoiding the pitfalls of having too many cooks in the kitchen?

Optimize: Which one or two strategies from the end of the chapter will you incorporate into your practice to improve collaborative decision-making, and how do you plan to implement them?

Lesson 14

Leading Change

"A good coach will make his players see what they can be rather than what they are."

—Ara Parseghian

Among all the things leaders are asked to do, one duty has risen to the top in terms of most difficult to accomplish with great success: *managing change*.

Far too many leaders see their attempts at change fail because they lack the patience to go through all the steps needed to effectively lead change.

In the modern workplace, top-down directives hardly translate to successful change. Whereas yesterday's generation blindly accepted marching orders, today's employees crave context, purpose, and voice.

Collaboration—not mandates—fuels lasting change.

> In the modern workplace, top-down directives hardly translate to successful change.
>
> Whereas yesterday's generation blindly accepted marching orders, today's employees crave context, purpose, and voice.
>
> #EdLeadershipPlaybook

* * *

Like many leaders, I originally struggled managing change. Upon reflection of my early years as a school administrator, I cringe at how poorly I led change efforts in my buildings.

While working as a middle school assistant principal, I spearheaded the implementation of a new policy requiring students to wear ID lanyards. Not understanding the complexity of leading systemic change, I recklessly emailed faculty over the summer telling them to be prepared to enforce these new protocols upon returning.

My assumption was that teachers could easily enforce these new rules in their classroom. *"How hard could it be?"* I figured. *"They're just lanyards."*

However—because I failed to engage employees in the change process—the new policy was a complete disaster. Students hated wearing the lanyards, and teachers felt little motivation to hold students accountable. This resulted in adversarial relationships between faculty and administration, which killed workplace morale.

Similar scenarios unfold in every school district. Leaders often decide that a change is necessary and implement it quickly, without considering the effort required to ensure a smooth transition. And when the change fails, they blame employees rather than reflect on their own shortcomings.

In his book *Work the System*, Sam Carpenter preaches the need to involve employees in the change process.

Carpenter—who was the founder and president of a nationwide telephone answering service company—estimated that 98 percent of his company's procedures were created by employees, while only 2 percent of the procedures were handed down by Carpenter himself. As a result, his employees were fully vested in these processes.

Carpenter speaks to a concept called *locus of control theory*, a subfield of psychology that suggests motivation is closely connected to whether or not people feel like they have control over their ultimate success.

Locus of control theory maintains that regardless of the inherent benefits, leaders who fail to involve employees in the change process shift their teams' motivation from internal to external, sapping motivation and making it unlikely that employees will support the change.

On the other hand, when employees are involved in the implementation of a change, and—just as important—are empowered to adjust as problems arise, internal motivation remains and change is much more likely to be embraced.

The following are nine ideas to effectively lead systemic change.

To be clear, change is complex and all situations require nuanced approaches. Therefore, these ideas should be viewed as *general principles* rather than *precise actions*:

Establish Relationships: Many books discuss change without mentioning one of the most important parts of the change process: *establishing strong relationships*. When asked to change their behavior, employees must trust that their boss has their best interest in mind. Leaders who invest time building social capital find change to be much more manageable than leaders who have done little to strengthen bonds with employees.

Seek to Understand Current Reality: Rather than assume change is necessary, leaders must seek feedback and truly understand employee perspectives. You can probably think of a freshly hired school leader who insisted on making sweeping changes without taking time to ask questions and understand the current reality. Unfortunately, this hasty approach often ends poorly for new leaders.

Honor Employee Readiness for Change: Once a leader has gathered enough anecdotal evidence, the best leaders seek data to support the case for change. While not all details will be known at this point, leaders would be wise to survey employees, asking whether or not they are ready for a change. Leaders should shoot for at least 60 percent support (better known as a *supermajority*) before moving forward, as anything less would be a disservice to employees.

Form a Committee: Effective leaders understand that top-down decisions are a recipe for disaster in today's workplace environment. Furthermore, the best leaders have the uncanny ability to make employees feel like a decision is their idea. To mesh these ideas, leaders would be wise to empower a group of employees to lead the change process. Depending on the significance of the issue, some leaders may want to remove themselves completely from the process and bring in a third-party consultant to facilitate the conversation.

For bigger changes, leaders may want to consider forming a committee.

Generate Employee Buy-In: In most cases, the committee will be a small representation of the larger group of individuals affected by the change. Therefore, proposed changes must be presented to the broader audience for feedback. While gathering input from all affected employees could be difficult, simply giving staff an opportunity to see the plans *before the change is announced* helps employees feel like a part of the process, thus increasing support.

Give Leaders Final Say on Proposal: Once a proposal for change has worked its way through the committee, leaders should have the opportunity to give the final blessing on the plan. Administrators should avoid shredding the plan to pieces—which would undermine the value of the committee—but rather look for small tweaks and revisions to ensure the plan is feasible.

Explain the Change: Once it has been determined that a change will be made, leaders must communicate the *why* and the *how* to employees. Why is a change being made? What is the timeline for a change? How will employees be impacted by the change? While some changes feel like no-brainers, there will always be employees who push back on change. Open and transparent communication is one of the best ways to keep even the harshest critics quiet.

Communicate and Give Time to Prepare: Once a change has been outlined, leaders must share details of the plans with employees. Whenever possible, leaders should communicate the changes to employees both in person (meeting) and in writing (email). Furthermore, leaders must give employees time to prepare for the change. In most cases, there is little reason to rush change.

Leaders who give plenty of lead time on changes find that employees are more supportive and more likely to buy into the change.

Revisit Changes and Make Tweaks: One of the best tips for leading change is to remind staff that changes are always reversible. I often use the lines *"Remember, this isn't a life sentence"* or *"We can always adjust if necessary"* when trying to convince employees to support change. This approach lightens the mood and helps get people who are on the fence over to your side. However, this can't just be lip service; you truly must be willing to discuss how change is going and what tweaks need to be made.

Machiavelli once said, *"There is nothing more difficult . . . than to take the lead in the introduction of a new order of things."* [17]

My experience confirms that leading change is the most difficult—and the most complex—responsibility of the school leader.

However, leaders who are structured and methodical with their approach often find that organizational change can be transformative.

Questions for Discussion:

Reflect: Think about an experience you had leading change. What aspects of the process went well and what aspects did not go as planned?

Apply. How might you use the concepts from this chapter when leading systemic change?

Balance: Considering the guiding principles at the end of the chapter, how might you apply these principles flexibly and adapt them to suit the specific challenges of your change initiative?

Optimize: Which step at the end of the chapter resonates most with you and how might you integrate it into your leadership practice?

Lesson 15

NO SURPRISES

"Leadership is a matter of having people look at you and gain confidence, seeing how you react. If you're in control, they're in control."

—TOM LANDRY

When I accepted my first superintendent job, I wasn't sure what to expect. To prepare for the role, I reached out to several current and former superintendents asking for advice.

While arranging these conversations took work, the advice gleaned during these discussions was priceless. We covered many topics, including administrator evaluation, program assessment, instructional leadership, and public relations.

However, one conversation in particular will always stand out. During a phone call with a retired superintendent, I asked him to share his best school leadership "rule of thumb." When I asked him the question, he paused for a moment, and then said the following:

"No surprises."

After another pause, he continued:

> *When facing a major issue, you must keep the board and your administrators in the loop. You must guarantee they are never caught off guard, and you must avoid making decisions that leave them scratching their heads. In turn, they should limit their surprises as well. It all comes down to no surprises . . . you must create a culture of no surprises.*

In theory, the concept of "no surprises" sounds simple. In practice, creating a culture of "no surprises" is far from easy.

※ ※ ※

Surprises come in all shapes and sizes and originate at all levels of school leadership. Surprises typically start with a school leader saying *"By the way . . ."* and end with an unexpected request or demand. Examples include:

"you have an IEP meeting today after school."

"you will teach a new course second semester."

"you have a student teacher starting next week."

"you need to sell tickets at the game tonight."

"you have a new student starting today."

"you are moving buildings next year."

To administrators, these may not seem like big deals. *"Teachers will just have to adjust"* principals declare prior to changing teacher lunch schedules or implementing a new classroom walkthrough template. While some staff go with the flow and adjust on the fly, most employees react poorly to surprises.

Consider the science behind surprises. According to *Surprise: Embrace the Unpredictable and Engineer the Unexpected* by Tania Luna and LeeAnn Renninger, surprises magnify emotions by as much as 400 percent.[18] When surprises are positive, the resulting happiness feels four times stronger compared to the same event without the surprise. Alternately, when surprises are negative, the resulting unhappiness feels four times as intense.

This is where school leaders must be very careful. Whereas many bosses believe their surprises will benefit staff, oftentimes they have the opposite effect. *"Why wouldn't employees want to be recognized in front of the faculty?"* and *"Why wouldn't our at-risk team want another counselor?"* were two surprise decisions I made as a high school principal that flopped.

As a high school assistant principal, I will never forget when we decided to hold a last-minute pep rally for our football team. Our team was in the middle of the state playoffs—and while we already held a pep rally for the first-round game—there was mounting student pressure to hold a pep rally for the second-round game.

Always a sucker for school spirit, I convinced our leadership team to cut 8th period by 20 minutes so we could gather in the gym to give our football team a fitting farewell. *"Why wouldn't teachers want to end class 20 minutes early?"* I assured the other administrators.

So as the last lunch shift wrapped up, I got on the loudspeaker and announced, *"By the way . . . we are having a last-minute pep assembly for our football team. Please bring your class to the gym at 2:40pm. Go Trojans!"*

Assuming I had made their day easier, I visited several classrooms shortly after the announcement. But instead of excitement, I noticed frustration on teachers' faces. *"I'm giving my 8th period a test. What am I supposed to do?"* asked one teacher. *"This is the third time you've shortened 8th period in the last two weeks,"* said another. *"You've had two pep assemblies for the football team, but nothing for our music programs,"* said a third.

The more classrooms I visited, the more I realized my "surprise" had backfired. What should have been a cool moment for our students was diminished because of added stress given to our teachers.

Tro-Jan Na-Tion! *Former NFL player JJ Moses hypes up the pep assembly crowd.*

※ ※ ※

What steps can leaders take to limit surprises? Consider these six ideas:

Brainstorm: When decisions are imminent, cycle through every individual who could potentially be impacted by the news. Even seemingly small decisions—such as when meetings are scheduled or how to order classroom supplies—could create issues if leaders do not look at each decision through a "who-could-be-surprised-by-this-news" lens.

It Goes Both Ways: When limiting surprises, the natural tendency is to consider employees we supervise. However, school leaders must also consider their supervisors. Most supervisors do not like being surprised with news. Catch them off guard too many times, and supervisors start to wonder if they hired the right person. Always remember that no one determines your career trajectory and professional fate more than your direct supervisor.

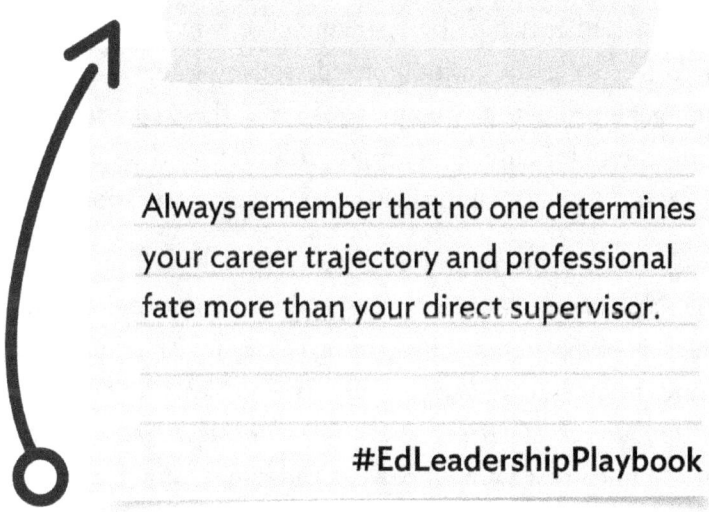

Always remember that no one determines your career trajectory and professional fate more than your direct supervisor.

#EdLeadershipPlaybook

Ask for Feedback: One simple step to avoid surprises is asking questions. *"What do you think about this idea?"* is a powerful question. Bosses who constantly ask employees for feedback on ideas eliminate the surprised feeling when decisions are made. Furthermore, leaders who actively pose questions and seek input find that staff are more supportive of decisions.

Don't Wait: Reduction in force. Plan of assistance. Realignment of duties. Administrators are responsible for having difficult conversations with employees. Fearful of upsetting their staff, many bosses wait until the last minute to share bad news. While some information must remain confidential, the general rule of thumb is the earlier you communicate and the more informed your people are, the better they'll be able to handle change.

Explain Tough Decisions: School leaders are notoriously bad when it comes to explaining tough decisions, especially personnel decisions. Rather than tell subpar employees why they are being moved to a different position or tell aspiring leaders why they didn't get a promotion, many bosses avoid these conversations all together. Not only is this approach unfair to the employee, this creates a culture of mistrust within the organization.

Apologize: Did you make a decision that took staff off guard? When this happens, one of the best things you can do is take ownership of the mistake. Apologizing is one of the most powerful gestures in the human arsenal. Leaders who have the courage to say, *"I'm sorry . . . I screwed up . . . I won't make the same mistake again,"* build trust with employees and can win over even the harshest of critics.

Having spent several years thinking about surprises, I've developed the following theory:

"People only get upset when they are surprised."

Think about this phrase for a moment. When you feel most upset, what are the root causes?

My son took the car without asking.
My daughter is failing a class.
My boyfriend cheated on me.
My girlfriend made plans during the game.
My husband forgot our anniversary.
My wife maxed out the credit card.
My friend isn't coming to my wedding.
My colleague didn't show up for their shift.
My boss is making me work this weekend.

In every case, what is the root cause of unhappiness? *Being surprised.*

Bosses who establish a culture of "no surprises" bring stability to a profession full of uncertainty.

Questions for Discussion:

Reflect: How do your current practices align with the principle of "no surprises"?

Apply: How might you apply the strategies discussed in the chapter to foster a culture of "no surprises" within your leadership approach?

Balance: How might you effectively respond when unexpected surprises for your staff arise, despite your best efforts to prevent them?

Optimize: Considering the ideas from the end of the chapter, what changes can you make to better ensure your staff is consistently informed and prepared?

Lesson 16

OPTIMIZE EMAIL

"Your ability to communicate to your people will determine your success."

—JIM HARRICK

Do you recall sending your first email?

Perhaps you were one of the earliest adopters, using America Online to send your first email in the early 1990s. Perhaps you were like me, using Hotmail (username *redhott818*) to send your first message after the service began in 1996. Or perhaps you've always been a Gmail person, sending your first email sometime after Google's 2007 public launch.

As is the case with most technology, email's impact on the workplace draws mixed reviews. When used properly, email increases workplace efficiency, provides a running record of communication, and keeps employees connected. When misused, email stifles employee productivity, produces underlying stress, and undermines organizational health.

Email was intended to make our work lives easier. Whether or not that is the case . . . well that's debatable.

You've got mail.

※ ※ ※

Let's be honest: email has completely transformed the workplace.

Before email, communication relied heavily on written memos, phone calls, and face-to-face interactions. Information dissemination took more time, and collaboration opportunities were more limited.

With email, leaders can very quickly and easily stay in contact with employees. Email allows leaders to disseminate information, provide updates, coordinate schedules, and organize meetings with the push of a button.

Email has improved the decision-making process. Email allows leaders to gather input, engage in dialogue, and quickly announce decisions. And during times of crisis, leaders can quickly share updates with large numbers of individuals.

Furthermore, email has improved communication with parents and external stakeholders. Email allows leaders to share news, celebrate achievements, and address concerns with individuals who are not physically present on their campus.

In addition to all of the typical benefits, email offers two "under-the-radar" benefits for leaders: *keeping documentation* and *respecting people's time*.

First, email generates *documentation*. How many times have you given staff verbal directives only to realize those requests remain unfinished several days later? Or, how many times have you shared instructions during a faculty meeting but later discover staff did not follow directions? Unfortunately, lack of employee follow-through plagues many organizations.

Having a paper trail is critical for holding employees accountable. Instead of debating what may or may not have been said in a conversation, email provides time-stamped evidence of marching orders. Shrewd bosses not only use email to efficiently communicate with large audiences, they also use email as a high leverage management tool.

Second, email is *respectful of people's time*. While occasionally leaders need a quick answer, the reality is most questions do not require an immediate response. Too many leaders interrupt others with nonurgent requests that could have been conveyed through email. Although these impromptu interactions only last a few moments, over the course of the week these disruptions add up.

My assistant sits approximately 20 feet from my desk. When questions arise, it's tempting to immediately visit her with every issue. However, doing so means I selfishly interrupt her work with my personal agenda. *Bosses—we are terrible at this.* Rather than disturb her concentration, sending an email allows her to respond when it's convenient for her.

***

While there are many positives, email also has its drawbacks.

First, email has resulted in information overload. The constant stream of incoming messages can inundate employees, making it difficult to prioritize tasks effectively. While intended to improve productivity and reduce stress, one could argue that email has done the exact opposite.

This leads us to time management. The pressure to respond to emails promptly can disrupt workflow and hinder concentration on more important tasks. Many leaders have erroneously created a culture of urgency—where employees believe they must immediately respond to emails.

Cybersecurity is also worth mentioning. Email has become a prime target for phishing attacks, exposing schools to data breaches and compromising sensitive information. These attacks have forced entire school districts to shut down, and are expected to be more prevalent in the future.

However, the biggest headache of email is *miscommunication.* Email can become incredibly toxic when it is not properly managed. The absence of nonverbal cues and tone in written text can lead to misunderstandings, conflict, and strained professional relationships.

Have you ever received an email that immediately rubs you the wrong way? Let's be honest—we've *all* been there:

A coworker blames you for a mistake.
A parent disagrees with your decision.
A supervisor criticizes your thinking.
A direct report denies your request.

Upon reading these emails, our heart rates rise, our muscles stiffen, and our blood boils. Our natural reaction is to immediately fire back with a scathing response pointing out why they are wrong.

For example, a few years ago a parent emailed me asking why I hadn't gotten back to an email they had sent three days prior. Almost immediately, I took offense to the message. *"If you think you know how to do my job . . . then go ahead!"*

I spent the next 60 minutes typing out (what I believed was) a perfectly crafted response explaining why I had yet to respond, while also reminding the parent of other *"urgent"* tasks consuming my time.

It took five minutes after pressing "send" to realize I should have stepped away from the email to let my emotions cool before responding. Not only would a phone call to the parent have been more appropriate, the stress it caused to write the email drained my body of precious energy needed to perform my job at a high level.

Unfortunately, using email to attack others has become commonplace in today's schools. Angry exchanges can erode workplace culture by fostering hostility and creating a toxic atmosphere of mistrust among colleagues.

Looking to improve your email experience? Here are nine ideas to consider:

Guidelines: Many employees don't know how to use email appropriately. Rather than waiting for issues to occur, leaders should facilitate a conversation where guidelines are discussed. Topics could include appropriate interactions with colleagues, open records laws for public employees, and expectations for emailing after work hours.

Courage: One rule of thumb I recommend for leaders is that all difficult conversations happen in person rather than through email. While they require courage, it's always preferable to convey unpleasant news face-to-face rather than through written communication.

Address Offenders: Every school has individuals who show a pattern of sending emails that attack and antagonize others. Leaders who want to maintain a positive culture must be willing to address these individuals, providing specific examples of their offenses and explaining that their behavior will no longer be tolerated.

Disconnect: Many school leaders believe they must always check and respond to work email outside work hours. *This is silly.* I recommend leaders actually *delete* the email app from their phone and only check email from their laptop. Deleting Gmail from my phone in 2016 was one of the best decisions I ever made.

Permission: Similar to their leaders, school staff also believe they must constantly be tethered to their inbox. *And we wonder why our employees burn out so quickly.* Leaders must remind staff that they have permission to disconnect from work—and, in the case of a rare emergency—they will be contacted by phone.

Positive: As an administrator, your email communication sets the tone for the entire building. Leaders who want to promote a positive environment should always strive for upbeat and supportive communication, assuming positive intent with their messaging while providing encouragement whenever possible.

Concise: If you've ever received a super long email, you know how overwhelming the feeling can be. Concise emails improve message clarity and enhance the likelihood of the message being read and acted upon. Furthermore, use spacing, bullets, and varied text (e.g., bold, underline) to increase the readability of your message.

Reply All: Strategically using "reply all" option can be a highly effective tool when it comes to promoting a culture of transparent communication and inclusivity. Reply all ensures that key individuals stay informed while reducing the need for duplicate messages.

Inbox Cleanse: One last psychological trick for email is the good ole inbox cleanse. Seeing a full inbox creates underlying anxiety and stress. To address this issue, leaders should set time aside to delete or archive all inactive messages while acting on all other dormant emails.

When I was young my dad once said, *"The older you get, the less fun it is to receive mail."*

I had never thought about mail this way. As a kid, getting mail (aka *snail mail*) was enjoyable. Whether it was a birthday card from Grandma, or the newest issue of *Sports Illustrated,* I was always eager to open the mailbox.

However, as we age, mail is mostly bills, notices, and junk.

The same thing could be said for email. During my *redhott818* days, new emails were met with anticipation. Whether it was a message from my girlfriend, or a trade request in fantasy football, email was exciting.

However, as we age, email is mostly questions, issues, and junk.

Let's flip the script on email.

Rather than allow email to complicate the workplace, administrators must take steps to ensure email does what it was intended to do—*make life easier.*

Questions for Discussion:

Reflect: How do your current email practices contribute to or hinder your workplace efficiency and relationships?

Apply: Considering the benefits and drawbacks of email outlined in this chapter, how will you ensure that your email usage enhances workplace efficiency and maintains positive professional relationships?

Balance: How might you determine which communications are best suited for email versus those that require face-to-face interactions to ensure clarity and effectiveness?

Optimize: Which one or two strategies from the chapter will you implement to improve your email communication, and how do you plan to incorporate them into your daily routine?

Lesson 17

DELEGATION

"You'll score a lot of goals in your career, but not one of them will happen without the help of a teammate."

—ABBY WOMBACH

My first day as an assistant principal was a whirlwind.

The day began at the district office where I completed paperwork and met district leaders. Next, I drove to my building where I was met by the head principal. After briefly chatting, we walked into the main office where I was introduced to several employees, including the nurse, counselors, custodians, and . . . my secretary.

"I can't believe I have my own secretary," I thought as I settled into my office. *"I've made it to the big time!"* At 26 years old, it was a surreal feeling knowing another adult's main purpose was to provide me with assistance.

However—only a few minutes later—exuberance turned to uncertainty.

"How exactly am I supposed to use a secretary?"

Despite having a master's in educational leadership, I quickly realized I had no clue how to manage the roles and responsibilities of another human being. Little did I know that being able to effectively delegate to others would be among the most vital—and most challenging—school leader responsibilities.

My dad used the harsh Minneapolis winters to teach me the basics of delegation.

Delegation is defined as the shifting of authority and responsibility for particular functions, tasks, or decisions from one person to another.

From a school leader perspective, delegation occurs when an administrator assigns specific tasks to their employees. By delegating those tasks to team members, administrators free up time to focus on higher-value activities while also giving employees increased workplace autonomy.

While it may sound simple, delegation is anything but easy. As much as they want to delegate work to others, many school leaders struggle to do so. A handful of core reasons exist as to why administrators fail to delegate. Consider the following:

"But it would take too long to explain the task."
"But I want to feel useful and need job security."
"But I enjoy completing certain projects."
"But I feel guilty about giving work to others."
"But I can't trust others to complete the work."
"But I'm the only person who can do the job right."

If you have used any of these lines, you are not alone. Most leaders justify their unwillingness to delegate using one of these reasons.

To combat this thinking, consider using The 80 Percent Rule.

The 80 Percent Rule is a delegation "rule of thumb" and reads as follows: *If there is someone who can do a task 80 percent as well as you can, delegate it.* Clearly, some tasks only administrators can do (e.g., employee evaluation, severe student discipline). However—in most cases—this rule can guide delegation decisions.

For example, as an assistant principal, I loved leading professional development. As an up-and-coming instructional leader, I felt great pride in teaching staff how to improve instructional practice. But upon moving into a head principal role, I quickly realized we had other individuals who were very talented—at least 80 percent of my capabilities—at leading professional development.

Another example was master scheduling. As an assistant principal, it was my responsibility to create the teacher master schedule. Not only did I enjoy crafting this important document, but I also relished having so much power over daily operations. But when I became a principal, I realized we had other individuals—such as assistant principals and counselors—who could also complete this task to at least 80 percent of my capability.

School leaders must recognize that the workload is immense, and it's impossible for one person to handle everything alone. The 80 Percent Rule helps administrators delegate less important duties so they can focus on more important tasks.

※ ※ ※

Looking to improve your delegation skills? Here are eight more ideas to consider:

Strengths: For most tasks, there's likely someone on your team with the skills needed to achieve the desired result. Leaders must always leverage employee skills by delegating tasks that play to employee strengths. Delegation gives others the opportunity to excel, which means employees are more motivated and engaged, thus increasing employee retention.

Time: Some people refuse to delegate when they consider the time needed to train another person. This thinking is misguided, as administrators should look at every situation through a *"how much time will this save me in the long run"* lens. Any time spent delegating on the front end will save loads of time on the back end, making delegation one of the most powerful, high-leverage activities in the leadership arsenal.

Power: Let's be honest, one of the biggest barriers to delegation is power. Despite the fact they are taught to be "servant leaders," far too many administrators are power hungry, believing they need to control everything that happens in their building. As Elsa says, *let it go.* Leadership is not about having power over others, but rather it's about using your influence to empower others.

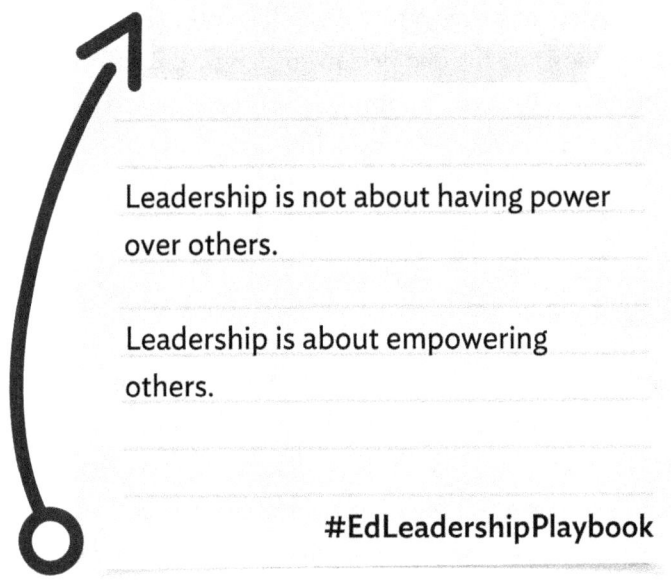

Leadership is not about having power over others.

Leadership is about empowering others.

#EdLeadershipPlaybook

Busy: Some employees argue they are "too busy" to assume new tasks. Unfortunately, all employees are busy. If we use "too busy" as an excuse for not taking on new tasks, nothing new would ever get done! In these cases, administrators must explain their thought process, identifying the work that is most valuable to the organization. This could mean that some work is pushed down to others, or eliminated altogether.

Compensation: This may be unpopular, but I believe administrators should always seek opportunities to compensate individuals who work beyond their normal duties. *"But Jared, there is no money in education!"* Baloney. My current district operates a $160 million budget. You're telling me you can't find a few hundred dollars to pay an employee who is delegated a new task? Gone are the days when we can keep adding duties to employee plates without either taking something off their plate . . . or increasing their compensation.

Secretary: As has been previously mentioned, the administrator's assistant must be a huge piece of the delegation puzzle. For example, my secretary controls my electronic calendar—dictating where I need to be each moment of the day. Furthermore, she takes care of virtually all my paperwork, state reporting, ordering, letters of support, and other routine tasks. Unfortunately, far too many leaders underutilize their personal assistants.

Support Staff: School leaders frequently miss opportunities to empower support staff. Incidentally, administrators who build capacity with paraeducators, custodians, food service, bus drivers, and other hourly employees often realize these individuals are eager to give more to their organization. It's amazing how potential blossoms when humans are trusted and given autonomy.

Follow-Up: An essential aspect of delegating tasks is documenting the agreement. Leaders face challenges when employees fail to fulfill their commitments, and without proper documentation, holding them accountable becomes difficult. Savvy leaders use email, Google Docs, and other electronic tools to record delegation decisions.

* * *

Individuals who move into school administration quickly realize they have a lot on their plate.

Those who refuse to delegate get stuck in the weeds and create massive inefficiencies in their organization.

Alternately, those who delegate build confidence in others while freeing themselves to do their most critical work.

Questions for Discussion:

Reflect: Reflect on your comfort level with delegating tasks to others. What specific challenges or reservations do you have when it comes to delegating?

Apply: How might you address those challenges to improve your delegation skills?

Balance: How do you balance between delegating tasks to empower and validate your team members while ensuring they don't feel overwhelmed or overburdened with too much responsibility?

Optimize: How will you apply the strategies from the end of the chapter to improve your delegation skills and ensure tasks are effectively and appropriately assigned?

Lesson 18

RUN GOOD MEETINGS

"If you want to win, do the ordinary things better than anyone else does them day in and day out."

—Chuck Noll

■ ■ ■

When I became an administrator, I immediately found myself leading many meetings.

Although I had led meetings in the past, most of them were informal conversations that impacted a small number of people. As a rookie building leader, I was now being asked to facilitate high-stakes discussions that would impact numerous students, staff, and families.

With little training on how to lead meetings, I relied on natural ability and gut feeling to run my meetings. Using this "fly by the seat of my pants" approach resulted in many issues.

First, my meetings lacked *purpose*. I was often unclear about the meeting objectives, which led to confusion from attendees and inefficiency in our discussions. The absence of clarity made it difficult to keep our team focused and productive.

Second, my meetings lacked *structure*. Unrelated discussions were common, leading us down rabbit-holes derailing our progress. Due to the loose structure of the meetings, valuable time and energy were wasted without reaching any solutions.

Third, my meetings lacked *collaboration*. One or two outspoken individuals would dominate the conversation, resulting in others feeling frustrated and useless. As the loudest voices drowned out others, important perspectives went unheard.

Finally, my meetings lacked *clear decisions*. Rarely did we circle back to our action steps, which led to attendees being confused on their roles. The lack of clarity resulted in minimal progress after the meeting concluded.

Consider the meetings you lead. Do they include purpose, structure, collaboration, and clear decisions?

Unfortunately, many school meetings lack these important pieces.

※ ※ ※

Administrators are asked to facilitate several types of meetings: faculty meetings, department meetings, parent meetings, and so forth. Moreover, one of the most common school leader meetings are "strategic" meetings.

Strategic meetings occur when a group of employees meet to discuss, analyze, and decide upon critical issues affecting the long-term success of the building. Examples include team leader meetings, department chair meetings, school improvement team meetings, and administrative team meetings.

As common as these meetings are, their outcomes are far from identical. Even within the same organization, strategic meetings can range from productive to pointless and everything in between.

What causes such a contrast in strategic meeting results? *The leader.*

Some leaders treat these meetings with the utmost importance, ensuring that their meetings are organized and productive. Other leaders treat these meetings with little regard, paying minimal attention to the finer details.

"Oh, it's just a meeting," you may be thinking. *"What does it really matter?"*

Leaders who accept bad meetings set a precedent for the rest of the organization. When tolerated at the highest levels, bad meetings become the ceiling of what can be expected in other meetings within the school.

That's not to say some employees won't try to make their meetings more effective than those of their boss. But it's unlikely they'll feel much pressure to do so. Contrast that with leaders who run fantastic meetings. Employees who leave well-managed meetings often feel compelled—if not pressured—to run their own effective meetings.

Think about the meetings you run. Where did you learn how to structure your gatherings? If you are like a majority of employees, your meetings are modeled after a current or former boss.

Always remember that your approach to running meetings could influence other meetings for years to come.

◦ ◦ ◦

Regardless of the type of meeting you are running, several "best practice" principles exist. Here are nine ideas to consider:

Clear Purpose: Every meeting must have a well-defined purpose, and participants should be sent the agenda in advance with an opportunity for input. This clarity ensures that time is spent productively and that everyone understands the meeting's objectives.

Encourage Participation: Educational leaders must actively engage all participants, encouraging them to share their insights, concerns, and ideas. The best administrators create an inclusive environment where diverse perspectives are valued.

Time Management: Wasting people's time is a cardinal sin of leadership. Therefore, meetings must start and end on time. The leader keeps discussions on track, preventing irrelevant conversations and excessive delays. Agendas are followed, and time is allocated appropriately for each agenda item.

Active Listening: Leaders must actively listen to participants. Rather than be preoccupied with their phone or laptop, administrators must acknowledge participant contributions, ask clarifying questions, and ensure that every voice in the room is being heard.

Positive Tone: Have you ever noticed how the tone of a meeting mirrors the leader's personality? Effective meetings maintain a positive and respectful tone, with a focus on *solutions* rather than *problems*. Leaders must be mindful of their behavior, setting an expectation for professional and courteous behavior.

Food: The presence of food at a meeting can play a surprisingly significant role in its success by fostering a sense of camaraderie and well-being. While not appropriate for every meeting, well-timed snacks can break the ice, encourage informal discussions, and promote a more relaxed and collaborative atmosphere.

Name a better combo—I dare you!

Transparency: Leaders must communicate transparently. Rather than withhold information, leaders must openly share all relevant details to ensure the team has the proper context for making decisions. Meetings are a prime opportunity for leaders to build relationships with employees.

Problem-Solving: Productive meetings focus on solving problems and making decisions. As the discussion unfolds, leaders must think about how they can guide their team toward an actionable outcome. When the meeting ends, attendees must be clear on next steps, as well as how decisions will be communicated.

Accountability: Leaders must ensure decisions are documented and establish a system for measuring progress while holding participants accountable to their commitments. Always remember: what happens after the meeting—as opposed to during the meeting—is the benchmark for productive gatherings.

Still not sold on effective meetings?

Many leaders complain about time spent in meetings. *"Why do we have so many meetings?"* they argue. The irony of this statement is a great deal of a leader's time is spent addressing issues that come about because *those same issues aren't resolved during meetings in the first place.*

As you think about the meetings you run, consider them not as time-consuming obligations, but as powerful tools for addressing the core issues that matter most to your school's success.

Questions for Discussion:

Reflect: Reflecting on the meetings you currently facilitate, how effectively do they incorporate principles such as clear purpose, active participation, time management, and accountability as outlined in the chapter?

Apply: How might you integrate the key principles discussed in the chapter into your approach to leading meetings?

Balance: What strategies do you use to balance thorough meeting preparation with managing your other job responsibilities effectively?

Optimize: Which specific strategies from the end of the chapter will you implement to enhance your practice in running effective meetings?

Lesson 19

TEACHER EVALUATION

*"Great players want to be driven.
Ordinary players want it to be easy."*

—Pat Riley

Great schools have a positive culture.
Great schools also have high expectations.

Whereas some people think it is impossible to have both at the same time, in reality this couldn't be further from the case: *the only way to have a positive culture is to have high expectations.*

And when it comes to blending a positive culture with high expectations, few things play a bigger role than teacher evaluation.

When discussing teacher evaluation, let's first discuss a traditional form of art known as mosaics.

Mosaics are known for the hundreds of unique colorful pieces arranged into patterns to create larger, singular decorative designs. Observers must be careful when looking at mosaics, as focusing on small, isolated parts of the artwork provides very little information about the bigger picture. Rather than jump to conclusions, observers must step back and look at how all of the small pieces work together to create a finished product.

Parallels exist between mosaic artwork and teacher evaluation. Rather than make evaluative decisions based on one snapshot of a teacher's work, administrators must reserve judgment until after gathering a comprehensive view of a teacher's performance.

The surprise classroom visit is a prime example of why leaders must resist making snap evaluative judgments. Most teachers have at least one "horror story" of an administrator classroom visit gone wrong. Whether students were misbehaving, the class was watching a movie, or the students had "free time"—a majority of educators can recall these moments.

I will always remember an unexpected classroom visit by my principal during my second year of teaching. Given the size of our high school (3,000 students and 200 teachers), it was rare for our principal to visit my classroom. However—on this particular day—my principal visited while I was making a call on my personal cell phone.

While the reason may have been legitimate (I was finalizing hotel rooms for an overnight trip for our cross-country team), the call should have been made at another time. So, when I saw the principal enter the room, I immediately hung up the phone, jumped to my feet, and reengaged with the class.

Once he left, I was terrified. *"What bad luck,"* I thought to myself. *"He probably thinks I'm a terrible teacher!"*

Later that day I visited my principal's office to apologize and explain why I was on my cell phone. To my relief, he was understanding of the circumstances and promised to visit another time.

How leaders respond to witnessing bad moments speaks to this "mosaic" idea. While most administrators are willing to collect more evidence before forming an opinion, some administrators make snap judgments based on one teacher interaction.

"Teacher evaluation must be ongoing."

If you've worked in schools for any period of time, you've likely heard this statement. Instead of receiving feedback only during the annual review, teachers should be given regular performance feedback. In short, *teachers should always know where they stand.*

Performance feedback can take a number of different forms. Formal classroom observations, informal classroom walkthroughs, email feedback, handwritten notes, and in-person conversations are all opportunities to provide staff with performance feedback.

Unfortunately, I have spoken with countless employees who indicate they "never" hear feedback from their administrator.

"Oh, come on," I respond. *"Surely, you must get feedback from time to time?"*

"Nope," they argue. *"In fact, I can't recall the last time I had a meaningful conversation with my supervisor about my work."*

If administrators aren't spending time with employees, what exactly are they doing? Studies indicate the average school leader spends more than 80 percent of their day engaged in "managerial leadership" tasks such as student discipline, supervision, email, paperwork, and phone calls, leaving little time for providing performance feedback.[19]

And when leaders do have time, they mistakenly assume performance feedback is unnecessary. *"My teachers know where they stand,"* some leaders say, believing their faculty are aware of their strengths, weaknesses, and general performance levels.

"Besides," these leaders argue, *"they don't want to hear from me. They just want to be left alone."*

The data would disagree.

Whereas 96 percent of employees appreciate hearing regular feedback from their employer, more than two-thirds of employees report not receiving enough feedback.[20] Furthermore, research suggests that the younger the employee, the more feedback they desire.

When administrators get out of their offices and into classrooms, they often witness incredible teaching. However, many supervisors fail to provide teachers with feedback. Rather than tell the teacher *"You crushed the lesson,"* some school leaders assume the teacher already knows, and they simply move on with their day.

Whether the feedback is verbal, handwritten, or emailed, never miss an opportunity to tell your people they are amazing. Far too many employees question their effectiveness because they are deprived of positive feedback from a supervisor.

Delivering constructive feedback is more challenging, as very few people enjoy telling someone: *"You can do better."* What leaders must realize is providing immediate feedback on shortcomings gives employees an opportunity to correct the problem before it's too late. And while they might initially resent the feedback, employees who grow from professional critiques often report stronger relationships with their supervisors.

Beyond collecting comprehensive data and ensuring that evaluation is ongoing, here are eight more ideas to help administrators navigate teacher evaluation:

Team Approach: While only one administrator will actually write the evaluative document (more on this in the following chapter), multiple evaluators should be given an opportunity to provide input on a teacher's performance. Using more than one administrator helps prevent any potential biases, while also ensuring the feedback is balanced and objective.

No Surprises: Providing timely, constructive employee feedback eliminates the following cardinal sin: *writing negative feedback in a performance evaluation the employee has never heard before.* Not only is this unfair to the employee, this is a quick way for bosses to strain relationships. While deficiencies must be documented, the evaluative conversation is *not* the time to introduce novel concerns.

Negative Feedback: When substandard employees are evaluated, negative feedback *must* be written into the formal evaluation document. Many administrators will identify employee concerns . . . only to never formally *document* those concerns. Lack of documentation is a huge issue for leaders, and is a primary reason incompetent teachers remain in schools.

Time: Administrators who provide timely, specific feedback throughout the year should keep running notes of those conversations. By the end of the year, the collection of notes should serve as an excellent performance review document. Rather than write a new evaluation, supervisors save time by printing notes and using those documents to drive the annual review process. In theory, minimal time should be spent writing the end-of-year evaluation.

Go Easy: This may be a hot take, but administrators should avoid writing critical feedback on a high performing teacher's evaluation. Great teachers are often very hard on themselves, and seeing critical feedback on an official document could take years to overcome. Therefore, leaders would be wise to *verbally communicate* constructive criticisms, as opposed to writing their concerns on the end-of-year evaluation.

Likeability: Let's face it: students learn from teachers they like. Therefore, administrators must be willing to address teachers who have patterns of relationship issues with students. But rather than tell teachers *"you are mean to kids,"* administrators must find ways to quantify the subjective feedback they receive on ineffective teachers.

Simplify: Many school districts ask teachers to turn in elaborate portfolios or projects as proof that teachers are "meeting the standards." Not only is this silly, this is an embarrassment to the profession. Why give overextended teachers even more work to do? Administrators—*not teachers*—should be collecting evaluative evidence throughout the year.

Request to Drop Classes

Counselors should complete this form every time a student or parent requests that a student is dropped from a class.

Counselor Name

Your answer

Teacher Name

Your answer

Teacher Class

Your answer

Student Name

Your answer

Person Requesting Class Change
- ○ Student
- ○ Parent
- ○ Student and Parent

Reasons for Dropping Class

Your answer

Request to Drop Class Approved?
- ○ Yes
- ○ No

This form allows administrators to address teachers who have patterns of poor relationships.

In the educational landscape, a revelation surfaces: *positive culture and high expectations can coexist.* High-performing schools seamlessly blend both, fostering an environment where educators thrive amid lofty standards.

Administrators who master the art of teacher evaluation propel morale and expectations to unprecedented heights.

Questions for Discussion:

Reflect: Reflecting on the analogy of mosaics and evaluation, how do your current practices ensure a comprehensive view of performance rather than focusing on isolated incidents?

Apply: How can you integrate the concepts of comprehensive, ongoing, and constructive feedback into your current evaluation practices?

Balance: How do your current evaluation practices reflect a balance between high expectations and positive support? In what ways can you improve to ensure your evaluations are comprehensive, ongoing, and genuinely constructive for those you evaluate?

Optimize: What ideas from the end of the chapter might you implement into your evaluation practices?

Lesson 20

EMPLOYEE MANAGEMENT

"A coach is someone who can give correction without causing resentment."

—JOHN WOODEN

Look at any principal job posting and you're likely to see the following essential duties: *Manage the supervision and evaluation of employees.*

While most will gloss over this statement, understanding how to effectively manage dozens (if not hundreds) of employees is a school leader's most important—*and most difficult*—responsibility.

Employee management is the series of activities that ensure supervisors provide employees with clarity about job expectations, as well as regular feedback about whether or not those job expectations are being met.

While this process sounds straightforward, my experiences have proven otherwise.

I have made countless employee management mistakes during my administrative career. I have been accused of "harassing" some employees and "playing favorites" with others. I have been told I'm "too liberal" by some staff members and "too conservative" by others. Throw in several teacher grievances and multiple lawsuits . . . and one might wonder how I still have a job!

At first, I felt alone in my struggles: *"Do I really have what it takes to effectively manage adults?"* I wondered as another "fierce" employee conversation went sideways. However, the more I discuss this subject with other administrators, the more I realize I am not alone: employee management is a *universal issue*.

This begs the question: Why is employee management so difficult?

The first reason is lack of training. Despite their best efforts, college instructors struggle creating scenarios wherein students feel the emotional weight of navigating a prickly personnel matter.

Second, very few districts support their leaders with this important work. Rather than train principals on effective employee management, most districts focus administrative professional development on new initiatives, theoretical frameworks, and flavor-of-the-day programs.

Finally, modern society makes employee management nearly impossible. Today's school culture expects principals to "play nice" with employees while also holding them to high—if not unrealistic—levels of accountability. However, push too far in either direction and stakeholders are holding pitchforks and calling for the leader's resignation.

Like a tightrope walker tiptoeing high above the city skyline, administrators must walk a fine line when it comes to employee management, as one small misstep could end in disaster.

"I have more than 50 employees in my building," you may be thinking. *"How can I possibly manage everyone?"*

Enter quarterly employee performance conversations.

Quarterly employee performance conversations are administrative team meetings where the work performance of every school employee is discussed. The word "team" is intentional because—as was discussed in the previous chapter—performance conversations are much more objective when multiple evaluators contribute to the discussion.

As a high school administrator, our administrative team (principal, assistant principals, and athletic director) used these quarterly conversations to manage our 100-plus employees. To guide our meetings, we used a Google Sheet where employee names were split into two groups (certified staff and support staff). As names were read, team members discussed strengths and weaknesses for each employee. After everyone shared their ideas and notes were recorded, we labeled each employee as a Tier 1 (highly effective), Tier 2 (effective), or Tier 3 (ineffective).

"Wow, that sounds intense!" you may be thinking. *"There's no way I could 'rate' our employees."*

While this practice may sound cold-blooded, understand these meetings were mostly positive and highly productive. My experience was that 90 to 95 percent of school employees fell into the Tier 1 or Tier 2 category. While their abilities ranged from capable to highly effective, we found that a large majority of staff were dedicated, hard-working, and passionate about kids.

While we could have spent hours discussing our effective employees, these conversations were limited due to the large number of people we needed to discuss. However, our administrative team made a commitment to ensuring our Tier 1 and Tier 2 staff heard consistent, positive feedback from our team.

So, what about the Tier 3 employees? These individuals were placed in one of two categories: *in need of informal coaching* or *in need of formal intervention*.

When our leadership team determined an employee had professional deficiencies, the first step was for that individual to receive informal coaching. This support was provided by an instructional coach, teacher mentor, administrator, or instructional supports outside the building.

Approximately two-thirds of employees who received informal coaching improved their skills to an acceptable level. However—for the employees who did not improve—the next step was formal intervention (more on this in the next section).

The primary benefit of these conversations is to ensure administrators keep employee work performance top of mind. Whereas busy school leaders could go months without considering the job performance of staff, this process ensures that school leaders remain focused on this all-important topic.

Another benefit of these conversations is that they ensure the administrative team is in sync with their feelings about individual employees. Far too often, employees receive mixed feedback from a principal who tells them they are doing "great" while the actions of an assistant principal suggest otherwise. This process helps ensure that employees know where they stand with their full administrative team.

Finally, a third benefit of ongoing performance discussions is that they hold administrators accountable for handling low-performing staff. Far too many leaders refuse to address underperformers and then wonder why they experience the same personnel issues year after year. By documenting agreed-upon action steps, colleagues are held accountable for addressing their assigned employees.

※ ※ ※

At some point in their career, all leaders will supervise an underperforming employee. While never fun, having the courage to address these individuals separates great leaders from the rest.

The following are ten basic principles for dealing with subpar employees. These methods have been endorsed by educator associations, referenced by legal firms, and were featured in *School Administrator* Magazine.

To be clear, *by no means should the following be considered legal advice*. When dealing with employee issues in your school, consult with your human resources department or district legal counsel.

Documentation: Documenting employee concerns is a critical responsibility for school leaders. Unfortunately, many administrators lack the awareness and patience to summarize and record specific actions related to employee underperformance. In today's overly bureaucratic world, schools must collect evidence to justify employee coaching and dismissal.

Patterns: Supervisors must focus on patterns of underperformance as opposed to single events. Aside from severe ethical and safety concerns, supervisors are required to document a series of infractions before jumping to formalized intervention. The cumulative nature of the infractions provides evidence needed to justify further remediation.

Working File: Typically maintained electronically by the employee's direct supervisor, the *working file* serves as a temporary holding place for coaching conversations and minor employee violations. When an employee's performance or behavior warrants formal intervention or discipline, documentation should be moved from the working file to the personnel file.

Personnel File: Typically a physical file in the district's human resources department, the *personnel file* serves as the employee's official work record. Significant employee concerns should be placed in this folder. Keeping all documented paperwork in one location supports future discipline-related decisions and becomes valuable during leadership changes.

Coaching Conversations (Step 1): Leaders must provide continuous support to all employees. When supervisors notice performance deficiencies, they (or a designee) must engage employees in *coaching conversations.* These discussions aim to develop new skills, refine existing ones, and help employees meet performance standards. Coaching documents should be placed in the employee's *working file.*

Awareness Phase and Verbal Warning (Step 2): An elevated notice of employee performance or behavior, the awareness phase and verbal warning are secondary intervention steps. The *awareness phase* addresses competency-related issues, while the *verbal warning* responds to behavior-related issues. Both documents should be placed in the employee's *working file*.

Plan of Assistance and Written Warning (Step 3): When employees are nonresponsive to coaching or their conduct is serious in nature, the plan of assistance and written warning serve as the most severe types of intervention. The *plan of assistance* is an official notice of persistent substandard performance while the *written warning* is used to document extreme behavioral misconduct. Both documents should be placed in the employee's personnel file.

Annual Evaluation: Annual evaluations reflect a complete picture of employee performance, meaning uncorrected below-standard performance must be identified in this document. As previously discussed, the annual evaluation should not be the first time the employee is made aware of deficiencies. Annual evaluations should be placed in the employee's *personnel file*.

Signature: Do employees need to sign corrective documents? While there is no "legal" requirement, it is best practice to have employees sign and date remedial documents to establish a clear record of receipt. In the event an employee refuses to sign, the evaluator could write the following: *"On (Date), I handed this document to (Employee) who refused to sign acknowledging receipt. (Evaluator Signature/Date)"*

Dismissal Hearing: As the "victim mentality" continues to pervade the modern workplace, leaders must be methodical in keeping accurate documentation of employee intervention. When personnel issues reach dismissal hearings, schools must establish the employee did not respond to coaching despite being afforded several opportunities. Furthermore, schools must prove the employee is likely to continue underperformance in the future.

Before we finish, let's discuss district-level leadership. Just because this chapter has focused primarily on building leaders who supervise teachers, understand that these lessons also apply to superintendents who supervise building leaders.

Similar to teachers, a large majority of administrators do a terrific job. Not only do they pour their heart and soul into students and staff, most school leaders work endless hours to ensure their buildings run at high levels.

Despite their heroic efforts, it is common for school leaders to go months without hearing positive feedback from a supervisor. District leaders: How often do you deliver specific, authentic praise to principals? Did you know that the most effective leaders deliver five positive comments for every one negative comment?[21] If you were to track your positive and negative comments, what would be your ratio?

Switching gears, how often have you heard the following: *"Bad principals are so hard to get rid of"*?

Put simply, *that's BS.*

Sure, administrators have bigger egos, larger paychecks, and are more likely to seek legal action. But when compared to teachers, school leaders are actually *easier* to remove thanks to limited contractual protections and multiyear probationary periods.

Unfortunately, many district leaders lack the courage to address underperforming administrators. Rather than use the steps outlined on the previous pages, they use excuses such as *"They aren't that bad," "They are retiring soon,"* and—my favorite—*"They are untouchable."*

Listen, no underperforming employee is "untouchable." Quit trying to justify your lack of action and *do the work*.

Superintendents: Please don't complain about how "difficult" your job is when you don't have the courage to remove poor leaders. Your job is "difficult" because you're always cleaning up the messes left by the poor leaders you continue to employ.

> Superintendents: please don't complain about how "difficult" your job is when you don't have the courage to remove poor leaders.
>
> Your job is "difficult" because you're always cleaning up the messes left by the poor leaders you continue to employ.
>
> #EdLeadershipPlaybook

Kathryn Minshew, CEO and cofounder of *The Muse*, said the following: *"Done right, a performance review is one of the best opportunities to encourage and support high performers and constructively improve your middle- and lower-tier workers."* [22]

Effective employee management provides school leaders with an opportunity to recognize the strengths of high-performers, while developing plans to support underperformers.

Administrators who stay focused on employee performance create a culture of continuous improvement within their faculty.

Questions for Discussion:

Reflect: Reflecting on your experiences both as an employee being evaluated and as a supervisor managing others, how have these experiences shaped your approach to evaluation and supervision?

Apply: How might you use the concepts from this chapter to improve your practices to better support and develop your team?

Balance: How can you balance maintaining high standards with offering supportive and constructive feedback in your evaluation and supervision practices?

Optimize: How might you apply the principles at the end of the chapter when dealing with underperforming staff to improve your current evaluation and management practices?

Lesson 21

DEALING WITH TOXIC STAFF

"Bad attitudes will ruin your team."

—TERRY BRADSHAW

In the previous chapters we discussed the importance of teacher evaluation and employee management. However, there is one type of school employee who deserves their own chapter: *the toxic employee*.

All schools have at least one person who sucks the positive energy out of the entire faculty. Whether we call them energy vampires, poisonous peers, or cancerous colleagues, the briefest interactions with these individuals leave us physically and mentally drained.

Repetitive dealings with toxic colleagues can have disastrous effects. Constantly being exposed to negative coworkers can lead to an increase in anxiety and depression and a decrease in motivation and engagement.[23]

Consider your current colleagues: Can you think of a notoriously pessimistic person who puts your stomach in knots whenever you're in their presence? Unfortunately, these employees single-handedly undermine school culture.

* * *

Early in my administrative career, I supervised a pair of teachers who worked closely together.

One teacher was positive, creative, and full of energy. She was loved by colleagues, and students enjoyed being in her classroom. In addition to being an incredible teacher, she was always looking to improve and welcomed coaching.

The other teacher was negative, prickly, and lazy. She isolated herself from peers, and students hated going to her class. In addition to being a subpar teacher, she thought she knew it all and resisted coaching.

One afternoon, the "positive" teacher asked for a few minutes of my time. During that conversation, she expressed discomfort working with her "negative" teammate.

She described the intimidation she felt working with this individual; moreover, she indicated new ideas were quickly shut down by her veteran colleague. She also shared that her coworker spoke poorly of her to others.

As our discussion concluded, the positive teacher indicated she *"dreaded coming to work,"* admitting she was considering leaving at the end of the year. It was during this time I reassured her that I would immediately address her concerns.

However, when I visited the negative teacher's classroom the following afternoon, she was already gone for the day. The next day, she was home sick. And the subsequent week was busy with school events. I kept finding reasons (okay, excuses) to postpone the conversation.

Truthfully, I was afraid of how the negative teacher would react to my feedback. The positive teacher wasn't exaggerating when she said her colleague was intimidating—we were *all* intimidated by her!

In short, the conversation never took place.

Two months later, I heard devastating news: The positive teacher accepted a job in a nearby district.

Shortly after hearing this information, I went to her room to offer my congratulations. Furthermore, I needed to know one thing: *Did my failure to address the toxic employee lead to a rockstar employee's resignation?*

Sure enough, her main reason for leaving was the personality conflict with her coworker. The situation had not gotten any better—only worse—since we talked.

My heart sank. I had completely failed one of our best employees. As a leader, this should have never happened.

If toxic employees are so awful for the work environment, why do they persist in our schools? Put simply, *leaders aren't doing their job.*

While they may feel comfortable discussing objective performance data such as test scores and attendance rates, many school leaders find it challenging to address subjective behavioral data such as employee attitude and colleague perceptions.

Leaders must recognize that behavioral accountability outweighs results-based accountability. Why? *Because employee behavior issues typically lead to poor performance outcomes.*

Think about your current coworkers. Are your pessimistic colleagues producing substandard outcomes? While there are always outliers, personal conduct typically drives professional results.

Unfortunately, some leaders believe the best way to address toxic staff is by asking teammates to address a coworker. *"Your team just needs to stand up to them,"* is a common phrase used by school leaders.

> Leaders: Stop telling employees "you need to have the courage" to address negative and toxic teammates.
>
> That is your job, not theirs.
>
> #EdLeadershipPlaybook

While in theory this sounds reasonable, in practice this is unfair. What employee wants to challenge a toxic teammate when they have to sit beside this person on a daily basis? Leaders alone must summon the courage to address negative employees.

What does a coaching conversation with a toxic employee look like? Here are six steps to consider.

Evidence: Most bosses go into meetings with toxic employees with little to no specific evidence outlining the problematic behaviors. Remember, toxic employees thrive on confrontation and are skilled at defending themselves in the face of criticism. Prepared bosses have several data points ready to defend their position when the bullets start flying.

Delivery: Telling someone their attitude needs an adjustment is no fun. The more we anticipate the employee's angry reaction, the more we want to avoid the conversation. If the thought of sharing hurtful (yet vital) information makes you sick to your stomach, consider the following: The intense discomfort in difficult conversations lasts an average of only *eight seconds*.[24]

Expectations: Once the message is delivered and tempers start to cool, the leader must develop clear expectations for the employee's interactions with others. Even if the toxic employee is in denial (which very well could happen), the boss must be very specific about the behaviors the employee must resolve moving forward.

Document: Delivering the message verbally to the employee is not enough. Leaders must document difficult conversations for the purpose of evidence when similar issues arise in the future. Sending an email to the employee summarizing the conversation should suffice. Unfortunately, many leaders lack the discipline to document these conversations.

Line in the Sand: Do you ever leave a corrective conversation with a toxic employee feeling uneasy because you're unsure if the recipient truly absorbed the message? *Don't worry.* As long as the message is delivered and documented, you have sent a shot across the bow that their harmful behavior will not be tolerated and any future misconduct will result in greater consequences.

Removal: If coaching and intervention do not result in transforming the employee's negativity, the boss may need to consider removing the employee. While not the easiest task to complete in the complex and bureaucratic world of education, savvy leaders realize eliminating even one toxic employee can transform a building's culture.

※ ※ ※

A couple years later, I spoke with the principal at the neighboring school where the positive teacher had landed. By every indication, she was thriving. Not only had she assumed leadership roles within the staff, she was perceived as a top teacher in the building. *Talk about pouring salt in the wound.*

Failing to address this unresolved conflict was one of the biggest mistakes of my leadership career. I learned that you will lose good people when you don't immediately confront toxic behavior.

Do not make my same mistake.

Rather than dodge difficult conversations, leaders have a responsibility to address toxic employees with clarity and resolve.

Questions for Discussion:

Reflect: Reflecting on your experiences with toxic employees, how have these situations impacted your work environment and relationships? What actions did your supervisor take or fail to take that either supported or worsened the situation?

Apply: In what ways might you apply the concepts from this chapter into your practice?

Balance: How can you balance the need for addressing toxic behavior decisively with the need for maintaining a supportive and positive work environment for the rest of your team?

Optimize: Which of the strategies from the end of the chapter do you want to implement to address and manage toxic behavior more effectively in your current or future roles?

Lesson 22

CLASSROOM WALKTHROUGHS

"It doesn't matter what you're trying to accomplish. It's all a matter of discipline."

—WILMA RUDOLPH

Providing effective instructional leadership presents a challenge for every school administrator. In addition to managing schedules, hosting assemblies, and disciplining students, leaders are expected to possess the knowledge and skill to make a positive impact on the teaching and learning process.

While there are several activities they could prioritize—such as leading professional development, attending PLC meetings, or analyzing student data—one instructional leadership practice gives leaders the biggest return on investment:

Classroom Walkthroughs.

Getting inside classrooms: one of the most powerful professional practices for school leaders.

Walkthroughs are loosely defined as brief, informal classroom visits that give school leaders quick snapshots of classroom activities and operations.

The term "classroom walkthrough" is relatively new. While administrators have visited rooms for decades, it wasn't until the early 2000s when the expression began to take hold in American schools.

In 2003, Margery Ginsberg and Damon Murphy shared seminal research on the impact of classroom walkthroughs. In their *Association for Supervision and Curriculum Development* (ASCD) article, Ginsberg and Murphy identified five key benefits to walkthroughs . . .

Walkthroughs help administrators:

become familiar with teachers' instructional practices.
gauge the school culture and climate.
develop a team atmosphere.
establish themselves as instructional mentors.
model the value of learning to students.[25]

Beyond these factors, there are several other benefits to classroom walkthroughs.

First, walkthroughs improve administrator *perception*. When administrators visit learning spaces, they get a first-hand look at how their school operates. Not only can they observe teacher effectiveness, leaders also get a true feel for their building's culture. Furthermore, administrators who actively engage with staff and students solve smaller issues before they become bigger headaches.

Administrators who get into classrooms improve *decision-making*. Rather than rely on second-hand information and hearsay, administrators who witness building operations with their own eyes make smarter decisions. Moreover, school leaders who share personal observations when explaining decisions are much more likely to gain buy-in from stakeholders.

Walkthroughs help determine *teacher effectiveness*. Administrators who rely solely on a one-time-a-year formal observation do a huge disservice to teachers. Alternatively, administrators who visit classrooms several times develop a clearer picture of teacher performance. And for low-performing staff, documentation from multiple walkthroughs is optimal for plans of assistance and/or teacher removal.

Next, walkthroughs are ideal for increasing *teacher confidence*. Administrators should view classroom visits as a golden opportunity to highlight the specific strengths of their teachers. In a time when financial resources are limited and it's difficult to keep teachers around, few things improve retention better than well-timed, authentic, *positive* feedback from a supervisor.

> When it comes to employee retention, few actions are more powerful than telling someone "you make a difference."
>
> #EdLeadershipPlaybook

Walkthroughs serve as a great *reality check*. Classroom visits can be a humbling and eye-opening experience for school leaders who have forgotten the challenges of teaching. Before giving faculty additional work or complaining about how stressful *their* job is, administrators who visit classrooms are quickly reminded of the demands placed on teachers.

Finally, walkthroughs are *therapeutic*. When I am low on energy and have a headache, visiting classrooms is the perfect remedy. Leaders who prioritize walkthroughs often find that getting into classrooms is one of the most enjoyable parts of school leadership.

On numerous occasions, I have told staff that I could spend all day in their classroom. I'm not joking!

※ ※ ※

While walkthroughs are excellent for providing staff with instructional feedback, the extent to which leaders make it into classrooms is varied. Despite many administrators claiming, *"Instructional leadership is my top priority!"* studies reveal that administrators spend less than 20 percent of their day engaged in this practice.[26]

What are some tips for prioritizing walkthroughs? Here are seven ideas to consider:

Goal Setting: Setting numeric walkthrough goals is one of the best ways to ensure classroom visits happen. Depending on the year, our administrators set an annual goal of 100 to 200 *documented* walkthroughs. One common mistake is forcing walkthrough numbers on administrators. Instead of saying *"You will do 10 walkthroughs a week . . . or else!"* asking administrators to come up with target numbers increases the likelihood that goals are met.

Keeping Track: Once goals are set, administrators must develop a system for tracking their walkthroughs. One simple yet effective method is by creating a Google Sheet (spreadsheet) that includes teacher names (y-axis) and the walkthrough dates (x-axis). This format works especially well for administrative teams who want to evenly distribute their visits.

All Hands On Deck: Districts that are serious about instructional leadership create expectations for *all* licensed administrators to visit classrooms. Do you have a five-member administrative team? All five should be in classrooms. Do you work in a small district? Superintendents and curriculum directors should help pick up the slack. Walkthroughs must be a team effort, and should never be the work of one person.

No Perfect Template: Notice how we have yet to talk about one specific walkthrough template. After thousands of walkthroughs, I'm convinced that *narrative feedback* is better than most complicated walkthrough forms. Unless a district commits time (usually several hours) to train staff on how to interpret walkthrough feedback, complex templates leave teachers with more questions than answers. Instead, administrators should learn how to summarize their visits in a couple of short paragraphs, focusing on the actions of the teacher and the students.

Two examples of narrative feedback I've given in the past.

Stay Positive: While my narrative examples look fairly basic, in reality few administrators use this approach. Too often, administrators believe walkthroughs are a time to nitpick teacher actions. Not only does this approach destroy school culture, many faculty lose their professional confidence as a result. Given the sensitive nature of instructional feedback, districts must ensure administrators focus on positives while reserving critiques for low-performers.

Explain: Most administrators assume teachers understand how walkthroughs work. *This couldn't be further from the truth.* What data is being collected? What feedback should a teacher expect? How often will visits occur? Who will visit my classroom? How do walkthroughs impact evaluations? Administrators must take time to explain the walkthrough process to teachers.

Double Dip: Efficient administrators view classrooms as their second office. Rather than sit in the office to send an email or draft a letter, why not sit in a classroom to work on those items? One of my favorite tricks as a high school administrator was to complete a walkthrough and then grab a student *from that class* with whom I needed to discuss their behavior. Many administrators find that their productivity skyrockets when they complete managerial work in rooms.

※ ※ ※

Instructional leadership doesn't need to be complicated. Simply getting out of the office and into the learning environment is a great first step.

And the one practice that provides leaders with the biggest return on investment?

Classroom walkthroughs.

Questions for Discussion:

Reflect: Reflecting on your approach to conducting classroom walkthroughs, how effectively are you incorporating this practice into your routine to gain insights into instructional practices and school culture?

Apply: What adjustments could you make to improve the impact of your classroom visits?

Balance: What ideas do you have to ensure you balance the need for frequent classroom walkthroughs with ensuring that each visit remains meaningful and provides valuable feedback to teachers?

Optimize: Which tips from the end of the chapter will you implement to make the biggest impact on your classroom walkthroughs?

Lesson 23

TRUST YOUR EMPLOYEES

"The team, not the individual, is the ultimate champion."

—MIA HAMM

When I was a building principal, a teacher asked for a week off from work to take a family vacation.

Although visibly nervous, she did a great job providing her rationale. First, she explained that this could be the last time her children get to see their aging grandparents. Next, she indicated that sports commitments made it impossible to leave during winter and spring break. Finally, she clarified that she was willing to take three days of unpaid leave.

As the teacher spoke, several thoughts cycled through my mind.

On one hand, I understood the unwritten rule that teachers are expected to work when school is in session. I realized that in most schools—even schools within our own district—similar requests were often denied.

On the other hand, I knew this teacher well. Not only did she have a solid attendance record, I also knew how much her family meant to her. And for her to relinquish three days of pay, this trip was clearly important.

When she was done speaking, I paused for a moment before saying these three simple words: *"I trust you."*

If my dad were not trusted to take vacation, we wouldn't have these fun family memories.

※ ※ ※

In education, the prevailing opinion is that employees should not be allowed to take vacation during the school year. This perspective is reasonable, as research outlines the connection between student performance and teacher attendance.

However, one can argue that another, more important variable is at play in this decision: *trust*.

Trusting staff to make decisions about taking time off is one small action that has a big impact on employee engagement. When administrators say "*I trust you*" to take time off, they are also saying "*I trust you*" in all aspects of your job.

That's not to say employees should be allowed to abuse the system. When approving extended absences, leaders should document the absence and inform the employee that similar future absences might not be approved. Furthermore, employees with poor attendance histories should not be granted the same level of flexibility as their more reliable colleagues.

Alternately, employees who have a proven track record of dependability should be trusted to make decisions about time away from work. Rather than avoid asking for time off in fear of their boss's reaction, employees should be empowered to use leave time and trusted to make the best decision based on personal circumstances.

In short, if staff are not trusted to make personal decisions—such as the best time to take vacation—then why would they go above and beyond in their everyday job? As leaders, our job is not to control staff, but rather to create an environment of trust.

> If staff are not trusted with vacation time, why would they go above and beyond at work?
>
> Effective leaders understand that trust—not control—is the secret to workplace productivity.
>
> #EdLeadershipPlaybook

"Building trust with employees doesn't seem like the best use of my time," you might be thinking. *"Aren't there other things I should be doing?"*

While school leaders are asked to do many things throughout the day, building trust must be a top priority. The following are nine reasons why administrators must invest time to build trust with employees:

Recruitment and Retention: A trusting culture is the ultimate magnet for attracting and retaining talented employees. Why? Because people are drawn to autonomous work. Trusting cultures inspire a sense of purpose, meaning, and contribution in their employees. School leaders who are serious about staff retention must create an environment where employees feel trusted and empowered.

Taking Risks: In a high-trust culture, people are 32 times more likely to take a responsible risk than they are in a low-trust culture. They're also 11 times more likely to innovate and 6 times more likely to achieve higher performance.[27] In a time where educating students has become increasingly difficult, employees must be given the confidence to try new things for the purpose of improving student outcomes.

Path of Least Resistance: Leaders who take time to build relationships with employees find that their jobs get much easier as a result. Bosses who fail to build trust discover that employees are naturally skeptical of decisions and are especially critical when mistakes are made. Alternately, bosses who build trust discover that employees are more supportive of decisions and are willing to forgive when mistakes are made.

Abundance > Scarcity: Far too many leaders today operate with a *scarcity mindset*. These controlling leaders think that their success is diminished when others are successful. A scarcity mindset leads to jealousy and an unwillingness to work with others. On the other hand, trusting leaders operate with an *abundance mindset*. These leaders understand that their success depends on others being successful. An abundance mindset leads to generosity and a culture of collaboration.

Follow the Leader: People who receive trust often feel inspired to pass along trust to others. Not only do employees who feel trusted return the favor by trusting their boss, they also follow the boss's lead by extending their trust to others. This "pay it forward" mentality results in a virtuous cycle of trust that ultimately impacts all employees.

Humility: Humility is widely misunderstood today; it is often seen as weak, timid, and soft—the opposite of real leadership. In truth, humility is enormously strong, courageous, and firm—the very essence of leadership. Humble leaders build trust by being more concerned about what is right than being right, about acting on good ideas than having the ideas, and about recognizing contribution rather than being recognized for making it.

Red Tape: Too often, leaders focus much of their time on rules and regulations as opposed to doing what is best for kids. Bureaucracy—a process designed to maintain uniformity and control within the organization—is one of the quickest ways to lose employee trust. Trusting school administrators value creativity over compliance and go to great lengths to remove red tape from their organization.

Chill Out: On rare occasions wherein freedom is abused, leaders must avoid overcorrecting. Far too many administrators create sweeping policy changes in response to a single employee mistake. Just as students should be treated fairly in the classroom, employees who consistently adhere to the rules should not be penalized for the inappropriate actions of a few.

Legacy: Think about a leader who exudes trust. It's immediately clear how much they stand out from the crowd. We feel a different level of energy when they enter the room. We feel a different level of commitment when they ask us to complete a task. Trusting leaders make everyone around them better, leaving a lasting legacy as a result.

Upon returning from vacation, I saw the aforementioned teacher standing outside her classroom. When asked about her trip, she immediately grabbed her phone and flipped through several pictures of her children with their grandparents. Her family created memories that will last a lifetime.

Not only did the teacher have a noticeable bounce in her step, but her positive energy lasted for months. Furthemore, this individual and I have had a strong relationship ever since.

Leaders who approach leave-time conversations with empathy—as opposed to skepticism—inch one step closer toward creating a culture of trust in their building.

Questions for Discussion:

Reflect: Reflect on a time when you felt trusted by a leader. How did that trust impact your motivation and performance?

Apply: In what ways can you encourage risk-taking and innovation among your team by fostering a trusting environment?

Balance: How might you balance maintaining necessary organizational policies while also allowing room for individual circumstances and decision-making in order to build trust?

Optimize: Reflecting on the considerations at the end of the chapter, identify one area of your leadership practice where trust could be improved. What specific actions can you take to strengthen trust and foster a more collaborative and empowering environment for your team?

Lesson 24

TREAT TEACHERS AS PROFESSIONALS

"The more honor and self-respect among players, the greater the team."

—FROSTY WESTERING

"Treat teachers as professionals."

Very often, this phrase is used in education.

Treating teachers as professionals means faculty are empowered to make their own decisions and are trusted to perform their job at high levels without being micromanaged.

Although they claim to treat teachers as professionals, districts often implement practices contradicting this statement. Consider the following expectations schools have for employees:

Lunch breaks are 30 minutes
Bathroom use occurs at set times
Family visitation is discouraged

Cell phones are off-limits
Daily attire is regulated
Leaving requires permission

I'm sorry, are we talking about school . . . or prison?

It may seem counterintuitive, but giving employees choices on workplace attire creates a culture of professionalism.

One litmus test for teacher treatment centers on medical appointments.

Say a teacher needs to leave work an hour early to take their child to the doctor. When given this request, administrators generally respond one of two ways.

Some leaders assume *negative* intent. These leaders mistrust their staff and believe employees have a hidden agenda. These leaders belittle staff, making it clear that it's not okay to miss work.

Finally, these leaders view requests through a bureaucratic lens, worrying more about the policy than the person.

Other leaders assume *positive* intent. These leaders trust their staff and believe employees have no hidden agenda. These leaders empower staff, making it clear that it's okay to miss work. Finally, these leaders view requests through an empathetic lens, worrying more about the person than the policy.

The key idea here is autonomy. *Autonomy* is the degree to which a job provides employees with the discretion and independence to go about their work. In autonomous work environments, employees have the freedom to make self-directed decisions without being micromanaged by administrators.

Studies suggest fostering autonomy in staff results in positive outcomes, including improved staff well-being, greater job satisfaction, higher workplace productivity, and increased employee retention.[28]

Of course, creating an autonomous culture does not mean administrators completely remove themselves from school operations. Leaders must strike a balance between giving employees latitude while also providing support. Rather than give employees unlimited freedom, leaders should develop general principles to guide employee decisions made in isolation.

What are some general principles that can help create an atmosphere of professionalism in your setting? Here are seven ideas to consider:

Policy Overhaul: Leaders should look at their policies and ask, "Does this rule exist because we don't trust some of our people?" If the answer is yes, you're likely annoying a large percent of your staff to prevent a few employees from misbehaving. Effective leaders seek opportunities to eliminate policies that restrict teacher autonomy.

90 Percent: My experience is that 90 percent of teachers are competent. So why do so many leaders worry about their "bottom" 10 percent when making decisions? Leaders must always base decisions on their best employees, while having the courage to privately address their worst employees.

Gray is Okay: Some leaders worry if they don't enforce rules, they will be viewed as "soft" by staff. While there is a fine line between being understanding and being a pushover, successful leaders in the modern workplace understand that not every situation is black and white, and it's perfectly fine to operate within the "gray."

Golden Opportunity: Given that most of their day is spent working with children, teachers have limited flexibility in their schedule. To compensate, leaders should give teachers freedom during "nonstudent" times such as before school and after school, as well as during professional learning and other contracted work days.

Work from Home: Speaking of being flexible, school staff should be allowed to work from home whenever possible. While remote work may not be feasible for all employees, effective leaders recognize that as long as work gets done at a high level, the methods (and location) for getting work done should not matter.

Patterns: Some leaders believe it is their duty to investigate leave requests and question employee absences. Not only does this take time and energy, this practice *kills* workplace morale.

Rather than worry about each individual absence, leaders should focus on attendance patterns and behaviors over extended periods of time.

Communicate: School staff are so conditioned to take orders, that when they hear a boss say, *"I trust you with this decision,"* employees assume there is a catch. To combat these misperceptions, leaders must take advantage of every opportunity to communicate their confidence in employees to make decisions without having to ask for permission.

Consider your current setting.

Are teachers treated as professionals?
Or, are teachers treated like prisoners?

Teachers have been micromanaged for far too long.

Let's stop telling teachers how to behave . . . and start letting them make their own decisions.

Questions for Discussion:

Reflect: Reflecting on your current leadership practices, how effectively do you treat your team as professionals by empowering them with autonomy and trust?

Apply: In what ways might you adjust your leadership approach to reduce micromanagement and foster a more supportive and professional environment for your team?

Balance: How can you balance granting autonomy with offering support to your team, and what guiding principles can you establish to empower team members to make independent decisions while ensuring alignment with organizational goals?

Optimize: Considering the guiding principles at the end of the chapter, identify one or two strategies you could implement to enhance autonomy and professionalism in your workplace. What specific actions will you take to integrate these strategies into your leadership practice, and what outcomes do you hope to achieve?

Lesson 25

INVEST IN CULTURE

"Find the good. It's all around you. Find it, showcase it, and you'll start believing it."

—JESSE OWENS

■ ■ ■

In *Delivering Happiness*, former Zappos CEO Tony Hsieh suggests the following:

"Once you have a culture—invest in it." [29]

Although this line is simple, it packs a powerful punch for administrators.

As school leaders, we learn to do more with less. We always search for ways to build culture using methods that don't cost money. We give notes of appreciation, allow staff to leave early, organize staff potlucks, and cover classrooms.

However, there comes a point when school leaders exhaust all their "free" ideas: one can only approve so many jeans days! In these cases, school leaders must dip into school finances for the purpose of *investing* in school culture.

But in a world where school purchases are increasingly scrutinized, how can leaders invest in school culture without getting slapped on the wrist by auditors?

Before we go any further, it's important to define school culture investments, as well as clarify the costs associated with these investments.

First, let's be clear that investments in school culture cannot be extravagant and must follow certain rules. Therefore, those hoping to take employees on a Royal Caribbean cruise or rent The Magic School (Party) Bus using district funds are out of luck.

Instead, we're looking at *strategic, occasional* instances when leaders provide gifts, facilitate activities, and organize gatherings that are modestly expensive for the purpose of enhancing employee morale and engagement.

"You said, 'modest expense.' How much are we talking?"

When discussing costs, it's important to understand school budgets. While school funding varies by state, in Iowa an average-sized school district (approximately 2,000 students) will likely spend in excess of $20 million in general fund expenditures.

The general fund covers all of the day-to-day operations of running a school district, including employee compensation, supplies, textbooks, professional development, and special programming.

The general fund also covers the "staff appreciation" purchases discussed in this chapter.

Given a $20 million budget, what would you guess is a reasonable percentage to invest in school culture? Five percent? Three percent? One percent?

While those numbers sound reasonable, they are likely far too much money to spend on these types of purchases. Believe it or not, spending *one-tenth of one percent* of the general fund budget—roughly $20,000—should be all you need to provide staff with meaningful perks throughout the year.

"Wow," you may be thinking. *"That's such a small percentage!"*

That's exactly my point! School leaders across the country run multimillion-dollar budgets. Yet, when asked to use school funds to buy coffee for the teacher's lounge they say, *"I don't think that's in the budget."*

※ ※ ※

Curious what could be done with $20,000? Below are seven ideas used in my previous school district of roughly 250 staff members:

All-Staff Celebrations ($10,000): We hosted four all-staff celebrations throughout the year. During these quarterly get-togethers, we served food, recognized employees, played games, and gave away prizes. Our staff relished this opportunity to connect with colleagues in a laid-back setting.

Staff T-Shirts ($3,000): Every staff member received a free T-shirt at the beginning of the year. We put a lot of thought into these T-shirts, including asking staff to vote on their favorite design and paying a couple extra dollars per shirt to get the ultrasoft-version (*Bella+Canvas* brand was our favorite!).

Flower Deliveries ($1,000): Our new teachers and certified staff were welcomed with plants delivered by our local florist on the first day of school. Each plant came with a specially designed pot with our school district logo. These gifts looked great in classrooms and helped new staff feel special.

Special Delivery: These school-themed plants were a hit with teaching staff.

Popcorn Fridays ($1,000): We purchased a popcorn machine for each school so that staff could enjoy a salty snack on Friday mornings. The delicious scent of fresh popcorn wafting through the office helped create a positive and uplifting atmosphere at the end of the week.

Family Movies ($1,000): Staff are always looking for something to keep their kids entertained during summer and winter break.

To help give our families something to do, we collaborated with our community theatre to host a free "staff-appreciation movie" for kids, grandkids, and spouses twice a year.

Pro Tip: *Let staff vote on the movie and the date of the showing.*

Yeti Mugs ($500): Our district emphasized lifelong learning, so staff who earned a master's degree over the previous school year were given a special Yeti tumbler with our school logo engraved. It can be challenging to find a gift that appeals to the masses, but these trendy mugs were a hit with everyone!

Baby Onesies ($300): We believed every employee (or employee's spouse) should be recognized for the birth of a baby. So, we ordered school-district themed "onesies" to give away during all-staff celebrations. Some staff said they wanted a baby just for the onesie (they were joking . . . I think!)

School-themed onesies are super cheap and cherished by staff.

Keep in mind these ideas are shared from a district perspective. Building leaders can use a similar rule of thumb for their buildings: For every 100 students, invest $1,000 of your building budget into employee culture.

Work in a 500-student elementary school? Invest $5,000. Work in a 1,500-student high school? Invest $15,000. Of course, you could go much higher if you wanted, but these numbers reflect an appropriate investment compared to the overall building budget.

■ ■ ■

"How are you able to do those cool things for staff? I didn't think we could spend money on those items."

Let's address this question from two perspectives: district leadership and building leadership.

District Leaders: When I began my first year as a superintendent, I was told "staff-morale" purchases such as food, clothing, prizes, and other "swag" were prohibited. However, I also knew that other districts were making these purchases without issue.

As I researched this topic, I discovered a crucial detail: auditors (the individuals who review and verify financial records) defer to school board policy when validating school purchases. Specifically, each district has an *"Expenditures for Public Purposes"* policy that governs allowable uses of school funds. Therefore, for our district to have flexibility on culture-building purchases, our public purpose policy needed modification.

Intrigued by the possibilities, I accessed sample board policies from the Iowa School Board Association (IASB) and the Iowa School Finance Information Services (ISFIS), searching for language that provided spending flexibility. I was happy to discover that these sample policies were far more flexible than our current policy.

One of the most helpful phrases came from ISFIS's sample policy and reads as follows: *"The Board of Directors authorizes the expenditures of District funds for . . . Motivational items for* employees that align with the Board's mission and vision for teaching and learning and enhance the climate and culture of the District."

Once drafted, the updated policy went to the school board for approval. Three key ideas were used as rationale during this discussion. First, I showed how the updated policy language came straight from state association guidance. Second, I shared research that spoke to the positive correlation between tokens of appreciation and employee retention. Third, I explained that far less than 1 percent of our general fund budget would be spent on these purchases.

After a short discussion, our board approved the new policy with a 5–0 vote.

Our full Expenditures for Public Purpose policy can be found on the South Tama County School District website. However, there are a few pieces of language I'd like to highlight:

> The Board of Directors authorizes the expenditure of District funds . . . which aid in recruitment of personnel, promotes improvement of staff morale and cooperation, and assists in building a commitment to the District, thus assisting in creating a more productive learning environment.
>
> Staff appreciation meals (breakfast and/or lunch) to recognize employee contributions . . .
>
> Motivational items for employees that align with the Board's mission and vision for teaching and learning and enhance the climate and culture of the district, provided the items are of modest expense.

District leaders should look at their current public purpose expenditures policy. If current language doesn't provide latitude, they should engage the school board in dialogue about modifying the language to allow for flexibility in spending.

* * *

Building Leaders: Similar to district leaders, building leaders should also investigate school board policy. Far too often, building leaders don't take time to understand school board policy, and instead rely on district leaders to interpret procedural language. When administrators dig into policy, they often realize their supervisor is misinformed, whether it be about public purpose spending or other policy.

Another tip for school leaders is to compose a public purpose statement for staff purchases that may raise a red flag in your business office. Once the statement is written and printed, those documents should be paperclipped to the receipt of the purchase in question.

Here is an example of a public purpose statement I've used in the past:

> *On Friday, August 23rd, the Tama Florist delivered an STC-themed pot and plant to all new certified STC employees. A total of 16 plants were delivered across all 4 buildings for a total cost of $770.40.*
>
> *I believe this purchase aligns with School Board Policy 804.07: Expenditures for Public Purpose. Specifically, I'd like to highlight the following statement: "Motivational items for employees that align with the Board's mission and vision for teaching and learning and enhance the climate and culture of the district, provided the items are of modest expense."*

My district credit card was used to make the purchase. Feel free to attach this email with the receipt in case the auditors have any questions.

Here is another email I shared with our business office to justify purchasing T-shirts for employees:

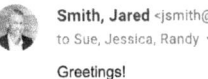

While this level of documentation may feel like overkill, referring to school board policy to justify purchases helps build trust with the business department while reducing issues with auditors.

In a world where effective school personnel are hard to find, leaders must look for opportunities to show staff appreciation.

Whereas apathetic leaders shrug their shoulders and accept that it's "impossible" to use district funds for staff morale purchases, determined leaders push forward and insist that funds be used to invest in school culture.

Questions for Discussion:

Reflect: Reflect on a time when you felt genuinely invested in by a leader or organization. How did that investment impact your motivation and engagement?

Apply: In what ways might you apply similar strategies as your leader from the example in your answer above to invest in and motivate your own team?

Balance: How might you strike a balance between making meaningful investments in school culture and adhering to budget constraints?

Optimize: Review the seven ideas mentioned for enhancing staff morale and engagement. Which one or two ideas could you implement in your own setting to effectively boost staff morale? How would you go about applying these ideas to maximize their impact?

Lesson 26

NAVIGATING A TEACHER SHORTAGE

"Never let your head hang down. Never give up and sit down and grieve. Find another way."

—Satchel Paige

When asked about the biggest challenge facing today's schools, one issue stands out: *the teacher shortage.*

Faced with this challenge, school leaders have two options: complain about the problem or look for solutions.

Those who complain about the problem say:

"Politicians need to give schools more money!"
"Colleges need to attract more students to the field!"
"Society needs to stop being so hard on educators!"

Those who look for solutions say:

"How can we attract more teachers?"
"How can we improve our hiring processes?"

"How can we keep teachers from leaving?"

Consider the phrases used in your setting:
Are you blaming others?
Or, are you taking ownership?

Unfortunately, many leaders do the former.

Compounding the issue, many school leaders place teacher recruitment low on their priority list. Rather than strategize how to attract highly talented employees, leaders prioritize test scores, student behaviors, mental health, and similar initiatives.

While all are important for school success, the previous statement poses a subtle irony: when schools hire effective teachers, initiatives have a way of taking care of themselves.

> When schools hire effective teachers, initiatives have a way of taking care of themselves.
>
> #EdLeadershipPlaybook

A few years back, I was in one of our buildings and saw a familiar face chatting with the building principal.

"Do you remember me?" this individual asked.

"Yes, of course I do!" I responded. *"You used to sub for us. How are things going?"*

"Well, that's why I'm here. I took a job at (a nearby district). Honestly, I don't like it there. I don't feel valued, and my opinion doesn't matter."

"You guys were different," they continued. *"You spent time getting to know me. And I was just a sub! It felt special working here. Everyone was so friendly and welcoming."*

"I want to come back."

The principal and I exchanged big grins. Not only did it feel good to hear how much of an impact our culture made on this person, it's not every day you have a teacher begging to work for you.

If you take nothing else from this chapter, let it be the following: *To be highly effective, today's administrators must possess a recruitment mentality.*

Having a recruitment mentality means two things: First, administrators must keep a constant pulse on their faculty so they can anticipate potential openings. Second, administrators must have a short list of individuals they can hire when openings arise.

How much time do you invest in subs, student teachers, and practicum students? Whereas some leaders say *"I don't have the time,"* forward-thinking administrators view these individuals as prime candidates to fill vacant positions.

The same could be said for interactions outside of work. School leaders who wish to keep their buildings fully staffed must approach every interaction through a recruitment lens.

One of my favorite stories to share is how I found a rockstar custodian at a Casey's convenience store. One winter morning, I was waiting in line to pay for my Monster Energy drink when a voice behind me said, *"Are you Dr. Smith?"*

I turned around and saw a middle-aged man who I had never seen before. He said he knew me from social media and had heard good things about my leadership. During our discussion, he shared that he was unhappy in his current job, and was looking at other options. Immediately, I went into recruitment mode and asked to exchange numbers so we could stay in touch.

Casey's: Famous for Pizza

A few weeks later, I texted him about a custodian opening in one of our buildings. Beyond simply alerting him of the position, I sent him the link to the online posting, passed along his name to our building principal, and told our HR department to be on the lookout for his application. Essentially, my goal was to remove all barriers that would prevent this individual from being hired.

One month later, he was introduced as our new custodian.

Whether it's the hard-working gentleman who stocks shelves at the grocery store, or the pleasant secretary who works at city hall, school leaders must always be on the lookout for talented individuals who could fill *any* workplace vacancy.

Some schools—especially those in large metropolitan areas—have their pick of the litter when it comes to hiring. As young singles prioritize living in areas where they have options for dining, nightlife, and social activities, these schools have the luxury of turning away droves of outstanding candidates.

If only all districts had this problem.

Nearly one-third of schools in the United States are located in "rural" areas with less than 2,500 residents.[30] Lacking the built-in amenities of their large-district counterparts, small districts face an uphill battle when it comes to alluring and securing strong applicants.

While rural schools have problems attracting teachers to their district, urban schools—especially those in low-income areas—experience high degrees of teacher turnover. This constant exodus of staff opting to work in more-affluent schools across town results in similar teacher shortages for inner-city schools.

Clearly, rural and urban schools have their work cut out for them in terms of attracting candidates to their districts. So, what steps can leaders take to address these issues? Here are nine ideas to consider:

Post Jobs Early: Starting the hiring process early is vital as schools battle over a dwindling number of qualified applicants. To get an accurate picture of the openings they will have the following year, districts should issue contracts as early as possible (in Iowa this day is March 15th). While they may not be legally binding, contracts are a major piece of the hiring puzzle that should be finalized ASAP.

Market Job Openings: Many schools use outdated approaches to promote teacher openings. Rather than passively post openings on job search websites, leaders must proactively market vacancies using social media and other forms of digital communication. In a time when teachers are in high demand, districts must ensure openings are seen by large audiences.

Be Aggressive: If you have ever been heavily recruited for a job, you realize how good it feels to be wanted. Turn on the charm and persuade candidates as to why they are needed in your building. Furthermore, consider sending "cold" emails, texts, and Facebook messages to potential candidates. I have sent hundreds of "Hail Mary" messages over the years, and—while only a handful have panned out—those positions would have gone unfilled had I not been persistent in finding candidates.

Provide Updates: No longer can employers sit back and refrain from reaching out to candidates for weeks at a time during the selection process. During hiring season, every day matters. Not only is poor communication rude to the applicant, there is a good chance another district will swoop in and secure the candidate when contact is not sustained. Simply sending a short text message letting the candidate know where you are in the process makes a huge difference.

Employee Referral Bonus: Do not underestimate word-of-mouth marketing when it comes to teacher recruitment. Research shows that 92 percent of people trust recommendations from friends and family more than traditional advertising.[31] In my previous district, we provided a $250 cash bonus to current staff who referred new teachers. By offering this incentive, employees were eager to alert friends of job openings.

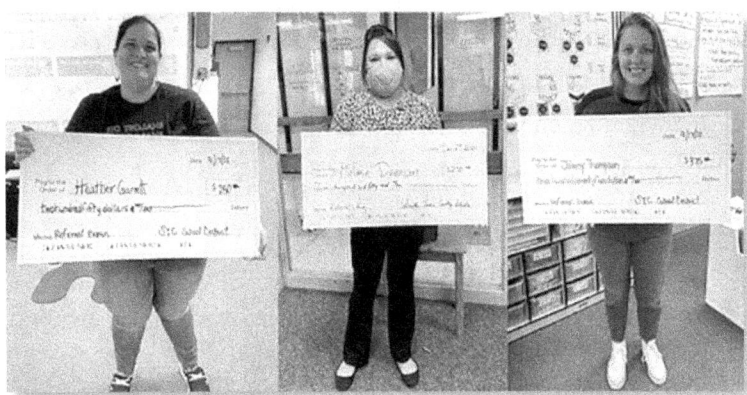

Our employees loved receiving these oversized "referral bonus" checks!

Empower Administrators: One of the biggest misconceptions in school leadership is that Human Resources is the only department that can discuss salaries with potential employees. Not only is this untrue, this practice creates massive organizational bottlenecks, slowing down the hiring process when time is of the essence. As long as they avoid promising candidates a precise income, leaders should not only be trusted to discuss salaries, they should be empowered to negotiate salaries using a set of clear guidelines.

Employee Check-In: Once a hire is made, the recruitment mentality should not stop. Administrators who are committed to keeping their buildings fully staffed must engage employees in retention-focused conversations. *"Are you happy in your current role?," "Do you plan to return next year?,"* and *"Are you looking at other jobs?"* are reasonable questions to ask. Leaders who take time to understand where each employee stands are rarely caught off guard by a surprise resignation.

Stay Interviews: We've all heard of exit interviews. But what about *stay interviews*? Rather than reactively ask employees why they are leaving, leaders should proactively ask employees what makes them stick around. *"What motivates you to work in our school?," "What could be better about your work experience?,"* and *"What opportunities within our district do you want to pursue?"* are questions that can take retention-focused conversations to the next level.

Career Goals Surveys: To gain a deeper insight into their professional aspirations, leaders should ask their staff to complete an annual career goals survey. By understanding the relocation possibilities, retirement plans, and leadership ambitions of their employees, administrators can tailor recruitment strategies to meet their building's staffing needs.

One topic that deserves its own section is employee compensation.

When school leaders propose teacher retainment solutions, the most common answer is to increase employee compensation. *"We just need to pay our teachers more money!"* administrators say, assuming compensation is the magic bullet.

Teacher compensation is undoubtedly a major concern, and school leaders must continue pushing educator salaries higher to ensure they are competitive with other professions.

However—when you examine the root cause of job dissatisfaction—compensation is rarely the primary factor. In a recent study examining the most common reasons employees leave a position, only 12 percent of employees cited, "wanting more money" as the primary cause for leaving a job.[32]

Rather than compensation, employees cited lack of flexibility, unempathetic bosses, team tension, lack of engagement, lack of appreciation, and lack of opportunities as bigger factors when leaving a position.

"Yeah, but schools are different," some readers may be thinking. *"When the district next door pays more money, employees will leave!"*

Research indicates across all professions it takes a 20 percent pay increase for employees to leave jobs they love. Alternately, it takes a 0 percent pay increase for employees to leave jobs they hate.[33] This means that a teacher making $50,000 would need to make $60,000 in another district to consider quitting.

Think about how your district salary structure compares to districts around you. Certainly, if you are paying teachers 20 percent less than the neighboring district, it's hard to blame teachers for leaving. However, my experience is that teacher compensation is fairly consistent across districts, meaning that money is rarely the deciding factor when employees choose to leave.

The lesson here is when employees feel valued, they're unlikely to leave just for a small pay increase at a neighboring district.

* * *

The challenges posed by the teacher shortage are undeniable.

However, by embracing a proactive recruitment mentality and establishing a culture of belonging, schools can transform themselves into magnets for talent.

Remember: The success of any school district is less about the selection of quality initiatives and more about the selection of quality individuals.

Questions for Discussion:

Reflect: Consider your current approach to recruitment. How have your actions and mindset affected your ability to attract and retain talent?

Apply: In what ways could you apply a proactive recruitment mentality to enhance your efforts and attract top candidates to your school or district?

Balance: How might you balance focusing on proactive recruitment with addressing current staff needs and morale to both attract new talent and retain your existing team?

Optimize: Which one or two of the nine recruitment strategies outlined in the chapter do you believe would be most effective in your context, and how might you implement them to improve your recruitment efforts?

Lesson 27

STAFF BURNOUT

"To be a top-class athlete, you have to train hard, you have to eat right, you have to get enough rest."

—Rory McIlroy

In education there is a long-standing belief: *The more hours you work, the better you are at your job.* Consider the following:

Administrators who work long hours are *"dedicated to their job."* Teachers who never leave school are *"committed to their work."* Staff who work through lunch are *"doing what's best for kids."*

Today's school leaders must grapple with the paradoxical reality of education; this is a profession full of passionate individuals who are prone to severe burnout. By ignoring this reality, administrators inadvertently perpetuate the culture of overwork.

Instead, leaders must remind staff of the dangers of overwork while also modeling healthy boundaries. Only *after* their leader prioritizes well-being will educators feel empowered to do the same.

Question: *Does working more hours result in greater productivity?*

Surprisingly, research shows people who work long hours are actually *less* productive than those who maintain 40-hour workweeks. Work more than 50 hours—as most administrators report they do—and efficiency worsens. Employees who work 50 hours only "produce" 37 hours of work, while employees who work 55 hours only "produce" 30 hours of work.[34]

This data is the crux of a philosophy I call *the 40-hour workweek mentality*.

A 40-hour workweek mentality prioritizes quality output over hours worked. When using this approach, leaders should tell their employees: *"You must work your 40 hours and get your job done at a high level. How you get there . . . well that's up to you."*

The benefits are clear: reduced burnout, boosted efficiency, and enhanced creativity. By trusting them to deliver within their 40-hour commitment, employees feel high levels of trust and autonomy. In turn, this allows staff to dedicate their energy to what truly matters on a schedule that works for them.

"This sounds great in business, but you can't do this in schools," you may be thinking. *"We have students to worry about!"*

Certainly, embracing a 40-hour workweek mentality in a profession with such prescribed hours can be challenging. However, administrators who wish to change the workaholic narrative must adjust their thinking about traditional work hours.

Consider a secretary who spends all night tackling a mountain of paperwork. As a result, this highly-motivated individual put in several more hours than their 8-hour workday suggests.

Under the 40-hour workweek mentality, this individual would have the freedom to leave work early on Friday to get a head start on a family vacation—assuming their job is being done at a high level.

Next, imagine an athletic director staying late on a Tuesday night to supervise a basketball game. While their contract hours suggest a normal 8:00am to 4:00pm schedule, this individual just completed a 12-hour day. According to the 40-hour workweek mentality, this individual should be given the flexibility to arrive at work late or leave work early later in the week—assuming their job is being done at a high level.

"That's easy for office staff," skeptics might say. *"What about teachers?"*

While teachers' schedules are less flexible due to having students for most of the day, school leaders can still apply the 40-hour workweek mentality. First and foremost, teachers should only be assigned work within their contracted hours. When school leaders implement new initiatives, they must allocate time for staff to complete work during contracted hours as opposed to assigning "home" work.

Second, leaders must ensure that teachers get protected planning time throughout the day. Teachers who work more than 40 hours usually do so for two reasons: lesson planning or grading work. Therefore, leaders must protect planning time (before school, after school, and during a teacher's planning period) as much as possible. While certain meetings (e.g., PLC, faculty) are often necessary, administrators should avoid taking away teacher planning time at all costs.

While this all sounds great, one major barrier to the 40-hour workweek mentality exists: *Perception*. In a culture where hard work is praised, some might raise eyebrows at secretaries who leave early, an athletic director who comes in late, or a teacher who follows students out the door.

Therefore, it is necessary to address these perceptions head-on. Administrators must remind employees of the 40-hour workweek mentality while also trusting employees to navigate their weekly schedule; the worst thing a supervisor can do is promote this approach while also questioning the whereabouts of their employees.

※ ※ ※

Another important topic to discuss is after-hours communication.

Many educators think they must remain glued to their phone in case *"something happens at work."* While at times true emergencies may arise, generally these matters can wait until the following day.

School leaders can't sit back and assume staff understand that after-hours communication is unnecessary. Instead, leaders must actively remind employees they have permission to disconnect.

One powerful method for reinforcing work-life balance is by facilitating a conversation about communication expectations. When employees have an opportunity to discuss timelines for responding to email, texts, and phone calls, they realize not every communication needs an immediate response. The end result of the discussion is a *communication protocol*—an agreed-upon timeline for responding to various modes of communication.

> Leaders can't assume staff know that after-hours communication is unnecessary.
>
> Instead, leaders must actively remind employees they have permission to disconnect.
>
> #EdLeadershipPlaybook

I have implemented a communication protocol as both a principal and a superintendent. While some of the nuances may vary, the gist of our protocol is as follows:

Email = respond within 48 hours (excludes weekends)
Text Message = respond that day
Call with voicemail or follow-up text = respond ASAP
Call without voicemail or follow-up text = respond as needed

Besides giving staff permission to disengage from their phone, this exercise allows teammates to hold each other accountable. Unfortunately, administrators are often some of the *worst* offenders when it comes to unhealthy communication.

While some bosses are overbearing and expect constant contact, others are difficult to reach, even during emergencies. Having a communication protocol holds all parties accountable to reasonable communication standards.

"But what if I enjoy work and don't mind working long hours," you may wonder. *"Is this wrong?"*

Some staff find great satisfaction in doing their job at high levels. These high performers not only produce great work outcomes, they also do an excellent job balancing life outside of work. Letting these employees proceed like normal is completely fine.

Personally, I feel a sense of purpose by doing my job well. Oftentimes, this desire to push myself professionally results in me working well past my 40 hours.

However, I have discovered I am most productive when I purposefully disconnect from work. Protecting my time on nights and weekends allows me to be hyperfocused and ultraproductive during the workday.

Nonetheless, school leaders must be cautious of people who have a reputation for consistently working long hours. Not only are staff who work unusually long hours typically less efficient than their counterparts, at times these people have ulterior motives for working extended hours. Such employees can be placed into four categories:

The Show Off: These employees love to brag about hours they work. They constantly remind coworkers in person and on social media about how many hours they complete.

The Complainer: These workers say they love putting in extra work . . . but then manage to find ways to complain about how much is on their plate. *You can't have it both ways.*

The Loafer: These people never leave work. These people also have low productivity. They may not show off or complain, but productivity levels do not match hours worked.

The Avoider: These staff say they love putting in extra work but don't appear happy or healthy. Often, these employees spend time at work to avoid dealing with issues at home.

In all four cases, leaders must have the courage to address these individuals. Left unchecked, these employees make colleagues feel inadequate for *"only"* working 40-hour weeks.

Beyond the thoughts shared above, here are seven more ideas to consider when combating staff burnout:

New Initiatives: As was previously mentioned, administrators should avoid giving employees work that can't be done during contracted hours. When leaders implement new initiatives, they must allocate time for staff to complete work *during contracted hours* as opposed to assigning "home" work.

Pay: At times, administrators will ask employees to complete tasks that must be done outside "normal" work hours. When this happens, administrators should consider paying employees for their time. While work expectations vary depending on employee group, administrators must remember that *time is money*; when employees are told to work nights and/or weekends, compensation may be necessary.

Planning Time: Although teachers are normally given planning time before school, after school, and during the day, in most cases this isn't enough time for teachers to get all their work done. Therefore, leaders should give teachers dedicated planning time on professional development days (more on this in the following chapter).

Our district now allocates 50% of professional development time for teacher planning.

Eat Lunch: One of the most common "badge of honor" educator behaviors is skipping lunch. School staff are notorious for working through lunch because they have "*too much work to do.*" Ironically, any time lost is more than made up for by skyrocketing afternoon productivity as a result of eating a healthy lunch.[35]

Positive Response: School leaders often make staff feel bad for taking personal days. Rather than dwell on the drawbacks of an employee absence, bosses should enthusiastically respond to requests while making employees feel comfortable about taking time off.

Model: Leaders become their own worst enemies when they encourage staff to take time off but never leave work themselves. Leaders: *Use vacation days and stay home when you're sick.* If you really feel compelled to work, fine; just do it from somewhere other than the office.

Be Careful: Management should be weary of attendance incentives. Although staff attendance and substitute shortages are a major concern in many districts, placing too much emphasis on absenteeism will result in staff feeling like they can't miss any time.

Leaders who understand the correlation between staff wellbeing and job performance must constantly remind employees that it's okay to disconnect from work.

Administrators who regularly communicate the dangers of burnout while giving staff permission to maintain a healthy work-life balance empower employees to reject the workaholic "*badge of honor.*"

Questions for Discussion:

Reflect: Consider your own beliefs and practices around work-life balance. How might your approach to balancing work and personal life influence the attitudes and behaviors of those you lead?

Apply: How might you incorporate the 40-hour work week mentality into your personal or professional life?

Balance: How might you strike a balance between being available for urgent needs and maintaining your personal time?

Optimize: Choose one idea from the chapter's list for combating staff burnout. How can you implement this idea to improve your practice or work environment? Outline the steps you'll take, potential challenges, and how you'll measure success.

Lesson 28

THE GIFT OF TIME

"We talkin' bout practice?"

—ALLEN IVERSON

As schools continue to adapt to new challenges, teacher burnout has become a hot topic of conversation.

Teaching has always been incredibly demanding. Now, we are asking teachers to make up for significant learning gaps, address a rise in student social-emotional issues, and—due to a nationwide substitute shortage—cover more classrooms than ever before.

It's no wonder teachers are leaving the profession in droves.

Unfortunately, some districts continue to march forward with strategic plans and new initiatives as if burnout is nonexistent. *"We've got to get our kids caught up"* leaders justify upon adding another task to teachers' already full plates.

But suppose you want to address teacher burnout. What practical steps can schools implement to address this important issue?

Better pay?
Improved benefits?
Self-care training?
Social gatherings?
Free yoga classes?
Bring puppies to work?

While I have tried every one of these ideas (yes, even bringing puppies to work), one gift stands alone when addressing educator fatigue: *the gift of time.*

"Bring Your Dog to Work Day" was one of my favorite traditions as a building principal!

Certainly, we could theorize the *gift of time* is important to staff. But what does the research say?

Gary Chapman is best known for his research on romantic relationships. In 1992, he published *The 5 Love Languages* which explored how couples express and receive love.[36] Chapman found when couples invest time to learn their partner's five unique styles of communicating love—*the five love languages*—they build stronger and longer-lasting relationships.

Given the enormous success of the Love Languages research, Chapman teamed up with Paul White to discover the keys to effective relationships at work. Called *The Five Languages of Appreciation in the Workplace*, the authors sought to help supervisors effectively communicate appreciation to their employees, which would result in greater job satisfaction, healthier relationships, and decreased burnout.[37]

Among their findings, Chapman and White discovered that *time* has become the most valued commodity for employees: *"For a while, 'time off' was seen as something that the younger employees primarily wanted. But we have found that 'time' has become the most valued resource for most employees, regardless of age group."*

Unfortunately, the educational system does the exact opposite of the research. Rather than trust staff to manage their time, administrators are notorious for micromanaging employees. Eight-hour workdays, canned curriculum, thirty-minute lunches, structured planning periods . . . schools are the *antithesis* of workplace autonomy.

Now when it comes to "time off," schools are admittedly limited in the amount of vacation time they can offer employees.

Given that most of an educator's day consists of actively engaging with children, teachers can't exactly come and go as they please.

However, school leaders must understand the psychological importance of time. Rather than throwing their hands up and saying, *"We run a school, there is nothing we can do!"* administrators must get creative in how they manage the workday.

※ ※ ※

One of my favorite professional practices is to complete 20-minute "rounding" meetings with teachers (see chapter nine). The purpose of these conversations is to create a safe space for sharing honest feedback, while also getting to know staff on a personal level.

In 2021—the first "normal" year after the pandemic—I began rounding meetings in September. Since school had just started, I assumed most teachers were still in the "honeymoon" period to begin the year. Unfortunately, the opposite was true. Not only were teachers reporting high levels of stress and fatigue, "burnout" was a common theme across my conversations.

The following are notes from a meeting with a middle school teacher, dated September 20th:

> *It's been so stressful. The kids are tough . . . and I'm being asked to cover classes . . . I just give so much of myself each day. There are days when I go home and just sit down because I'm exhausted. I don't know what it is, but I feel more tired and stressed than ever before.*

Here are notes from a conversation with a high school teacher, dated September 23rd:

This is my 16th year as a teacher. It's also been my most difficult. I feel as stressed as I would in December, and we're only five weeks into school. I am stressed beyond belief. The constant covering . . . it's really taking a toll. We need time. We need more time.

Regardless of building level or content area, the themes of stress, exhaustion, and fatigue kept popping up in our conversations.

Realizing we needed to quickly come up with a plan or risk losing staff (both figuratively and literally), a colleague and I brainstormed ideas that would show staff: *"We hear you."*

We discussed several ideas: offer mindfulness training, hand-deliver goodie bags, take staff to a movie, and bring in food trucks for lunch. But when the dust settled, one thought rose above the rest: *give teachers time.*

We generated a plan that would add one two-hour early dismissal each month for the rest of the school year. By having students leave early, teachers would gain much-needed planning time. To be clear, this was not additional planning time, but rather *protected planning time* we owed teachers who were constantly being asked to cover empty classrooms.

When we presented this idea during an all-staff meeting, our teachers were thrilled. Not only did they desperately need the planning time, they were ecstatic that we had listened and were honoring their feedback. And after reviewing a survey in which an overwhelming majority of employees favored the plan, it became clear that *time* is what staff wanted.

One small hurdle existed: school board approval. Given this plan would change the school calendar, we needed the school board's blessing on the idea. Nevertheless, after explaining the thought process, sharing the survey data, and providing answers to potential pitfalls (more on this to come), the school board unanimously approved our recommendation.

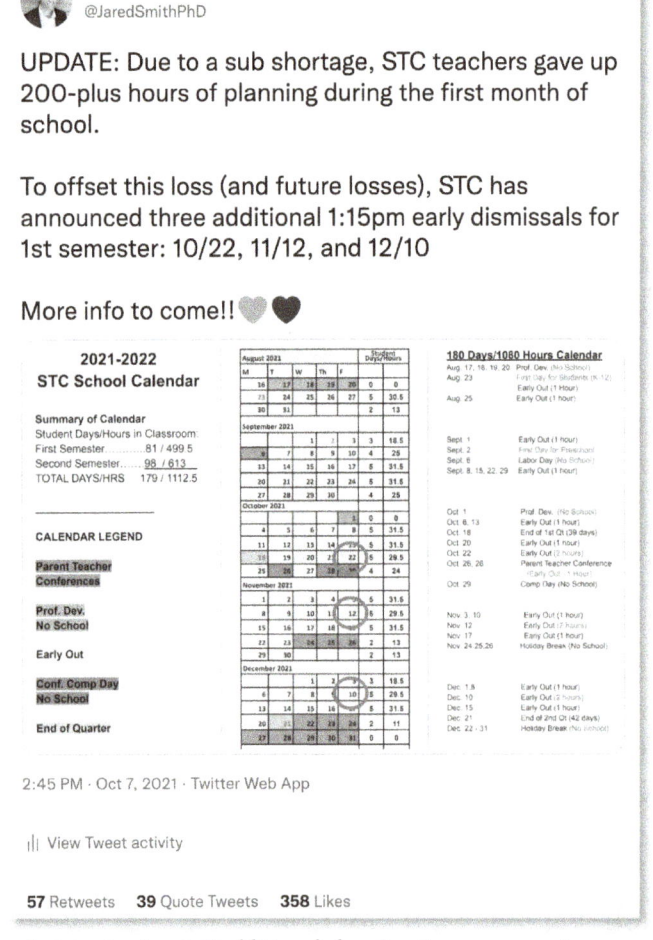

Our decision to give staff additional planning time was a rousing success.

When others heard about our plan, several questions emerged. The following were seven of the most common concerns, along with my response:

"What about student supervision?" Student supervision must be discussed any time a school considers adjusting the daily schedule. Assuming that leaving work was not an option for most parents, we arranged for paras to supervise students. We also asked our transportation department to run two separate bus routes: one at the early dismissal time (1:15pm) and one at the regular dismissal time (3:15pm).

"What about lost instructional time?" Philosophically, this was the most difficult question. The pandemic caused a year's worth of learning loss, so how could we justify giving up more instructional time? However, one could argue that whatever instructional time had been lost would be recouped when teachers were better prepared to teach the material and more motivated to perform their jobs at high levels.

"Will your staff abuse the time?" One more time for the people in the back: *Leaders must make decisions based on their best staff.* Unfortunately, too many administrators worry about their worst staff and make decisions for all based on the poor decisions of a few. This mindset results in schools never pushing forward with new innovations. Finally, if you have staff who you know will abuse time . . . *why are they still in your organization?*

"Won't your community complain?" Every community has individuals who complain about school decisions. While these people can be exhausting, understand that community perception impacts

the leader's influence. Rather than ignore the obvious obstacles of a decision, administrators should forecast potential questions and address those concerns when an announcement is made.

> Leaders must trust employees to make their own decisions.
>
> If your organization is full of people whom nobody trusts, then your organization is full of the wrong people.
>
> #EdLeadershipPlaybook

"But it's hard to collect data!" It's crazy to see how many districts make subjective decisions rather than collect objective data. Leaders must search for multiple data points to help justify difficult decisions. *"Yeah, but our staff hates surveys,"* you may be thinking. The reason most staff hate surveys is because leadership never bothers to use the feedback!

"Cool plan! But it won't work here." Why do so many school leaders lack the initiative to implement good ideas? *It's hard work.* The process of scheduling rounding meetings, encouraging critical feedback, brainstorming possible solutions, generating employee

buy-in, and implementing change takes time and energy. But isn't that what leaders are paid the "big bucks" to do?

* * *

Teacher burnout isn't going away.
In fact, it's only going to get worse.

While several options could help teachers, one solution rises above the rest:

The gift of time.

Questions for Discussion:

Reflect: Reflect on your own experiences with time management in your professional life. When have you felt most supported by having "the gift of time," and how did it impact your stress levels and productivity?

Apply: How might you apply the "gift of time" concept in your life or work? What steps will you take, what challenges might you face, and how will you measure the impact on well-being?

Balance: How can you effectively balance providing additional time for staff with the need to meet instructional requirements and student needs?

Optimize: Choose one or two common concerns from the chapter that are most relevant to your organization. How will you address these concerns to enhance your practices or policies?

Lesson 29

Handling Job Rejection

"Never give up! Failure and rejection are only the first step to succeeding."

—Jim Valvano

I spent eight years as an assistant principal.

Those eight years provided a great learning experience. I handled all of the "typical" AP responsibilities such as student behavior, master scheduling, nighttime supervision, employee evaluation, and instructional leadership.

While I enjoyed the role, like most APs I had a dream of one day running my own building. Having the opportunity to put my own "touch" on a school was very appealing.

During my time as an assistant principal, I applied for numerous head principal jobs. While other colleagues got their shot after a single interview, I wasn't having nearly the same luck.

I participated in several principal interviews. Each time, I came away thinking, *"This is the one!"* only to discover they had chosen another candidate.

It wasn't until my 11th interview when I was finally given a chance.

That's right, my first *10 interviews* ended in rejection.

※ ※ ※

Dealing with rejection can be difficult. Given most school leaders are accustomed to success, not being selected for an administrative job can be a humbling experience.

Unfortunately, going through several interviews before reaching the next level in school administration is typical. Whereas sometimes it appears leadership "gatekeepers" are playing a cruel joke, the reality is most jobs are highly competitive.

Like many others, I struggled with each rejection. I felt anger toward the interview committee and jealousy toward the person who was selected. Furthermore, I began to wonder if I had "what it takes" to be a head principal.

Worse yet, it was common for the local media to announce job finalists prior to the final round of interviews. In addition to the intense pressure I put on myself, the fact that *everyone* knew I had interviewed made it especially embarrassing when admitting I didn't get the job.

Despite these challenges, understand that *everything happens for a reason.*

HANDLING JOB REJECTION

> **Meet and greets planned with MHS principal candidates**
>
> Members of the public will have an opportunity to speak with two finalists interviewing for the position of Marshalltown High School principal this week.
>
> Jared Smith, assistant principal at East High School in Waterloo, and MHS Associate Principal Kenneth Hayes will be at the MHS Media Center Friday.
>
> Hayes will be available from 5-6:15 p.m., and Smith from 6:30-7:45 p.m.
>
> Jacque Wyant, principal at West High School in Sioux City, and Deb Holsapple, MHS associate principal, are also finalists for the position.
>
> Public forums with Holsapple and Wyant are to occur next week, but a date has not been finalized.
>
> Three interview committees are also scheduled to privately meet with Hayes and Smith Friday.
>
> The committees include MHS staff, MHS students, district administrators and community members.
>
> Interview committees' feedback will be submitted to Superintendent Marvin Wade, who will make the final selection. That candidate is slated to be presented to the Marshalltown School Board for approval at its next meeting, April 6. That date may change depending on interview schedules.

Ugh. How embarrassing to admit I didn't get this job!

Reflect on the jobs you haven't landed. Are you still upset? Or, are you thankful for the new path your life has taken? In most cases, people realize they are much happier with how things played out.

For me, one job stands out in particular. I had given a stellar interview and was certain I was the most qualified candidate. My confidence was so high that my girlfriend and I began house hunting! But after a couple weeks of hearing nothing (not even a phone call), I realized I didn't get the job. *I was stunned.*

But now that time has passed, I feel fortunate about the outcome:

My philosophy did not fit the district culture.
My personality did not mesh with district leadership.
My strengths would have been limited by the position.
My career trajectory would have been stifled.

Not getting a job can be a blessing in disguise.

Still struggling with professional rejection? Here are seven ideas to consider:

Take Ownership: We live in a culture where it is typical to blame others for our lack of success. While this feeling is natural, at some point as professionals we must take ownership of our shortcomings. Those individuals who use a growth mindset—understanding that there is always room for improvement—are much more likely to have success in future interviews.

Feedback: While employers are growing increasingly wary about giving feedback thanks to potential discrimination complaints, finding someone who can provide accurate, critical feedback is the best way to improve your interview approach. People who treat each failed interview as a learning opportunity discover that their interview skills improve exponentially over time.

Perception: When it comes to internal promotion, one of the biggest barriers is public perception. If you are finding it difficult to move up internally, it may be because people don't have a good perception of you. Have the courage to ask colleagues how you are perceived by others, and then commit to improve on areas of weakness.

Relocate: Are barriers in your current setting hurting your chances at promotion? It may be time to look outside the district. While kids and families make moving difficult, people who are determined to take the next professional step may need to broaden their search. Besides, you can always return at a later time.

Core Values: One of my most effective preinterview strategies is to spend time reflecting on my core values. I have found that articulating—in writing—my fundamental leadership beliefs helps ensure that these ideas are communicated during the interview. Want to really impress the interview committee? Give each individual a copy of your core values.

Silver Lining: What positives can be taken from *not* being selected? For starters, not getting a promotion means you likely have more time on your hands. Focus the energy that would have gone into the new job toward other parts of your life—such as family, fitness, travel, education, or hobbies. Taking time to list the *positive* repercussions of not getting a job can do wonders for your mental health.

Motivation: One of my all-time favorite quotes is: *"The best revenge is massive success,"* by Frank Sinatra. Once the sting has subsided, use rejection as motivation to push you even harder. Create a list of the jobs you haven't been given and promise yourself that those who didn't pick you will eventually realize their mistake. When used appropriately, few things are as motivating as rejection.

List of Job Rejections Since 2010

1. Fort Dodge Middle School Principal
2. Humboldt Middle School Principal
3. Fort Dodge Elementary School Principal (Cooper)
4. Western Dubuque Middle School Principal
5. Waterloo Middle School Principal (Central)
6. Union High School Principal
7. West Marshall High School Principal
8. Waterloo West High School Principal
9. Johnston High School Principal
10. East Marshall High School Principal
11. Waterloo Middle School Principal (Bunger)
12. College Community Middle School Principal (Prairie Creek)
13. Marshalltown High School Principal
14. Fort Dodge High School Principal
15. South Tama County Superintendent
16. North Cedar Superintendent
17. Southeast Webster Grand Superintendent
18. Okoboji Superintendent
19. East Marshall Superintendent
20. Tipton Superintendent
21. Des Moines Public Schools Director of Teaching/Learning
22. Carroll Superintendent

Prove the doubters wrong. Every. Single. Day.

Best-selling author and retired US Navy SEAL John "Jocko" Wilink once said the following:

How do I deal with setbacks, failures, delays, defeats, or other disasters? I have a fairly simple way of dealing with these situations, summed up in one word: Good.

Oh, mission got canceled? Good. We can focus on another one.
Didn't get promoted? Good. More time to get better.
Didn't get the job you wanted? Good. Build a better resume.
Got beat? Good. We learned.
Unexpected problems? Good. We'll figure out a solution.

That's it. When things are going bad, don't get all bummed out or frustrated. Just look at the issue and you say, Good.[38]

As painful as the process was, I am thankful I was rejected 10 times. Not only am I able to help others process their rejection, I am also better prepared to handle future rejection.

Rejection provides motivation.
Rejection opens doors.
Rejection gives perspective.

Next time you are rejected, remember one word: *Good*.

Questions for Discussion:

Reflect: Reflect on a significant moment of rejection in your career journey. How did it impact your self-perception and career trajectory at the time? In what ways has this experience shaped your approach to future challenges and opportunities?

Apply: How might you apply the concepts for handling rejection from this chapter to improve your approach to career setbacks?

Balance: How can you balance taking ownership of your career development with maintaining a positive perspective on setbacks and rejections? Consider how you can use both approaches to improve your professional growth and resilience.

Optimize: Which of the strategies for handling rejection listed at the end of the chapter can you implement in your approach to future job opportunities? Describe how you will use these strategies to enhance your chances of success and resilience during the application process.

Lesson 30

LACK OF EXPERIENCE

"Age is no barrier. It's a limitation you put on your mind."

—Jackie Joyner-Kersee

"We're looking for experience."

Aspiring school leaders hear this all the time when trying to move up the administrative ladder.

Whether you're a teacher trying to move into teacher leadership, an assistant principal hoping to become a head principal, or a principal wanting to become a superintendent, "experience" is often the barrier to landing a job.

Let's face it—this feedback stings. Not getting a job can be frustrating, especially when committees seem more concerned with your resume than your skills.

Furthermore, the *"lack of experience"* line poses a great irony: How is one supposed to have experience . . . if they are never given a chance to *have* experience?

※ ※ ※

Does experience really matter?

One study investigating the link between an employee's prior work experience and their performance in a new organization found no significant correlation between the two, determining that experience doesn't predict a new hire's success.

In *Rework*, Jason Fried and David Heinemeier Hansson suggest, *"There's surprisingly little difference between a candidate with six months of experience and six years. The real difference comes from the individual's dedication, personality, and intelligence."*[39]

Likewise, in *Good to Great*, Jim Collins reminds us: *"In determining 'the right people,' the good-to-great companies placed greater weight on character attributes than on specific educational background, practical skills, specialized knowledge, or work experience."*[40]

But what about schools? Does experience matter for educators and—in our case—educational leaders? With limited research exploring the connection between experience and effectiveness of school employees, anecdotal evidence is where we'll turn.

When leading interview teams and the "experience" discussion comes up, I often share the following:

> *"Think of the teaching staff in your building. Imagine you have a piece of paper. On the left side of the paper, every teacher is listed from most experienced to least experienced. On the right*

side of the paper, every teacher is listed from most effective to least effective. As you compare both lists, do you see any correlation?"

Committee members are often surprised to see there is little correlation between lists. In fact, some employees suggest there is an *inverse correlation* between both sets of names.

This same exercise applies to school leaders. Consider the administrators in your district, or the administrators you have worked with previously. If you created two lists—one in order of experience and one in order of effectiveness—would you see a connection?

It doesn't take a complex meta-analysis to determine there is *minimal correlation* between administrative experience and administrative effectiveness.

* * *

Despite little evidence confirming its importance, "experience" is normally high on an interview committee's list of preferences.

While interview committees know what they are getting with experienced leaders, inexperienced leaders are seen as wild cards. Even if the experienced leader is mediocre (as many well-traveled leaders are), interview committees often settle on a reliable veteran as opposed to gamble on a boom-or-bust rookie.

When interview committees look at inexperienced candidates, they often assume the worst-case scenario. Even when novice leaders interview well and show great potential, interview committees often second-guess their abilities.

"How are they going to handle (name of the most difficult employee in the building)?" committee members ask. *"They are going to get eaten alive!"*

"They've never dealt with students as bad as (name of the most difficult student in the building)!" they say. *"We need someone who can put their foot down!"*

The fear of an up-and-comer leaving after a few years is also a concern for some committee members. Believe it or not, someone being "too good" or "too talented" for the job is a common consideration.

"They are just going to leave us in a few years," these individuals say. *"It would be better to pick someone who isn't so ambitious."*

Unfortunately, these thoughts reflect a scarcity mindset. Rather than pick the best candidate with the belief they can keep them long-term—and replace them with another talented person when they leave—interview committees often select the safe choice, leading to years of pedestrian leadership.

※ ※ ※

While there is minimal data suggesting experience results in effective leadership, perception is reality. To combat these preconceived notions, here are seven ideas to help you shed the lack-of-experience stigma:

Resume Building: When considering dozens of applications, interview committees only have a few moments to inspect each resume. One thing they typically hunt for is relevant leadership experience. Candidates should list these roles at the top of the resume as opposed to burying them deep in the document.

Don't have many formal leadership roles? Do what you can to make them look formal. Are you a department chair? A mentor teacher? Assigned to special committees? Brainstorm and list leadership duties even if they don't have official titles.

Provide Examples: Let's face it, experienced leaders have more examples to share in interviews. When asked questions like "Share a time when you addressed a difficult employee" or "Tell us about your background with school budgeting," veteran leaders have a wealth of examples to draw from, while younger candidates struggle to deliver off-the-cuff responses. Novice leaders must come prepared to share examples demonstrating how their unique experiences translate to the administrative role.

Practice Makes Perfect: Because they've sat through more interviews, seasoned leaders are usually more polished as compared to their beginner counterparts. To close the gap, aspiring leaders should conduct practice interviews. Sample school leadership interview questions can be found online or by asking others for documents used in their district. Beyond verbally practicing answers, writing down responses to questions helps with recall during high-stress interrogations. Have a lengthy commute to your interview? Conduct a rehearsal interview during your drive.

Admit Your Weakness: While it may feel counterintuitive, consider tackling the "experience" stigma head-on in your interview. It is likely the interview committee has already discussed your lack of experience. *Own It.* During interviews, I would openly acknowledge that I was going up against individuals with more experience. I would then explain how my inexperience motivated me to learn and grow. *Being coachable* is one advantage that most novice leaders have over veterans, and is a concept that inexperienced leaders must highlight in their interview.

(Don't) Act Your Age: Like it or not, people have preconceived notions of what leaders should look like. Often, these leaders are older and more mature looking. *Yes, I'm telling you to look old in your interview.* Consider your clothing, your hair, and your makeup. Wear glasses and cover tattoos. Sick of getting shut out on jobs, I grew a goatee and landed a job on my first try. Similarly, a colleague who had similar bad luck shaved his head and immediately secured a new position. While these were likely coincidences, age can be an unconscious bias for many committee members. Finally, do you have a family? Use your spouse and kids to your advantage, as mentioning family makes candidates sound more mature.

The first known photograph of me with a goatee—it appears I aged five years overnight. Outdoor lighting may have also played a role.

Location, Location, Location: I have met numerous candidates who are fixated on working in large districts. *"There's no way I'm working in a small town,"* they claim. While I get the allure of the big city, understand that *bigger districts = stiffer competition.* While you may know people who landed big district jobs, it is likely they were an internal candidate, had connections, or lucked out with a shallow candidate pool. Understand that beggars can't be choosers and you may need to relocate to a rural district to get your foot in the administrative door. And once you get there, absolutely *dominate* so that others start to notice.

Let's Be Honest: You may not want to hear this—but sometimes committees use the "experience" line as an excuse for not hiring you. It's far easier to say *"We chose the candidate with more experience"* than *"Your interview was terrible."* With the legal system the way it is, employers often use the "experience" line to avoid potential lawsuits.

As an assistant principal, I was told numerous times *"We went with someone who had more experience"* as the reason I didn't get the job.

One time, I recall getting a rejection phone call on my way to the gym. Upset about getting passed over yet again, I crushed my workout while listening to Tupac's *"Hit 'Em Up"* on repeat (*listen at your own risk*).

Next time you are told *"We're looking for someone with experience,"* use this advice to come back stronger. And when you finally get your chance, use rejection as your motivation to perform your job at the highest of levels.

Questions for Discussion:

Reflect: Reflect on a time in your career when you faced challenges due to a perceived lack of experience. How did you respond to this situation, and what strategies did you employ to overcome it?

Apply: Considering the concepts from this chapter, how might you apply these strategies to current or future opportunities to address similar challenges?

Balance: In what ways might you effectively balance showcasing your existing leadership experiences with addressing any perceived gaps due to a lack of formal roles?

Optimize: Which strategies listed at the end of the chapter can you implement to address the challenge of lacking experience in your leadership journey? How will you apply these strategies to enhance your candidacy for future opportunities?

Bonus Lesson

GROWING LEADERS

"Each person holds so much power within themselves. Sometimes they just need a little nudge."

—PETE CARROLL

◼ ◼ ◼

A few years ago, I discovered that one of our administrators was being courted by a nearby district for an open position.

The neighboring district was three times our size, and the position would include increased responsibility and greater compensation. Despite being a promotion for the employee, my initial reaction was frustration.

"Those jerks!" I thought upon realizing a nearby district was recruiting one of our top employees. *"Who do they think they are?"*

My frustration also focused on our employee. *"What, are we not good enough?"* I complained. *"Besides, how are we going to find a suitable replacement in June?"*

Upon reflection, I realized my selfishness. Rather than focus on our organization, I was stressing over the actions of another district. And rather than do what was best for our employee, I was worried about the additional work that would fall on my shoulders.

As leaders, it is our responsibility to help employees reach their full potential. Rather than feel threatened or betrayed, our role is to help staff take their next professional step.

As leaders, our job is to create more leaders.

In *Multipliers*, Liz Wiseman says, *"The best leaders encourage people to grow and leave. And when people leave, they celebrate their departures and shout their success to everyone."*

Consider your current school district:

Does your district encourage professional growth?
Or, does your district hinder leadership potential?

Sadly, many school leaders feel resentful when they realize an employee is leaving for another district. Rather than understand this is the next step in their professional career—or reflect on the steps they could have taken to make the individual feel more valued—these leaders immediately blame the employee: *"They obviously weren't committed to our school,"* they tell others.

In the story I shared, the employee would move from a director position into an assistant superintendent role. Accompanying the promotion would be a 40 percent salary increase. *Would you turn down a 40 percent salary increase?*

But say the employee makes a lateral move. Instead of moving up the leadership chain, what if the employee accepts a similar position in a new school district? These are situations when leaders must self-reflect. Rather than get mad at the person for leaving or blame another district, bosses should reflect on their treatment of the individual:

Have I offered support, or have I ignored requests for help? Have I provided autonomy, or have I micromanaged their work? Have I invested time, or have I been too busy for the employee?

Ironically, more employees leave jobs as a result of the relationship with their boss than they do their level of salary.[41]

> More employees leave jobs as a result of the relationship with their boss than they do their level of salary.
>
> #EdLeadershipPlaybook

This concept of districts intentionally hindering leadership growth doesn't solely apply to external movement. Sadly, many districts are guilty of stifling internal leadership potential.

One common example is when districts prevent their best assistant principals from moving into head principal roles. In many districts, up-and-coming assistant principals serve under middling head principals. Rather than move the AP into a head principal role elsewhere in the district or—*heaven forbid*—remove the mediocre principal, district leaders keep gifted assistant principals in supporting roles for far too long.

Publicly, district leaders will say *"Oh, they're just not ready for a head role,"* while privately they think *"If we move them into a new position, their (current) school will fall apart!"* Rather than promote internal candidates, districts tell promising assistant principals *"Your time will come"* while keeping them in the same role year after year.

Furthermore, it is quite common for effective teachers, teacher leaders, and instructional coaches to be stonewalled from taking the next professional step in their very own districts. Rather than actively help teachers move into administrative roles, some supervisors lack a growth mindset when it comes to leadership development for their teachers. Whether the fear is *"they're too good in their current role"* or *"it'll be too hard to fill their position,"* many leaders worry about their own problems as opposed to focusing on how they can support the teacher-leader's growth.

While some employees patiently wait for their turn despite the politics, others become frustrated and leave the district. Quite often, these individuals turn disrespect into motivation, propelling them to highly successful careers.

※ ※ ※

What else should be considered with leadership development? Consider these six ideas:

Hire for Talent: Many leaders are leery of hiring highly talented individuals. Afraid the employee will leave after a couple years, they pass over the more gifted candidate to select the safer fit. This thinking is misguided. Leaders should always hire the most qualified candidate and then offer opportunities for growth and autonomy. In many instances, school leaders simply want to work in a district where they feel trusted and valued.

Job Security: Egotistic leaders sometimes worry that understudies are so good in their roles they could eventually find themselves without a job. Again, this thinking reflects a deficit mindset and kills trust between supervisor and direct report. Leaders should view skilled subordinates as conduits to growth while also preparing those individuals to take their next professional step. And if a go-getter lights a fire under a complacent leader, is this really a bad thing?

Next Person In: The fate of the administrator depends on the effectiveness of the team in which they surround themselves. Therefore, the best school leaders have a constant shortlist of individuals—both internal and external—they can contact when leadership opportunities arise. Rather than sit back and wait for candidates to apply, cunning district leaders treat leadership openings like gold and aggressively recruit potential replacements.

Promote from Within: In *Good to Great,* Jim Collins reminds us: *"Visionary companies have shown, time and again, that they do not need to hire top management from the outside in order to get change and fresh ideas."*[42] How often do you see school districts hire flashy outsiders for principal and district-level roles . . . only to see those individuals flame out in a few short years? Oftentimes, internal candidates possess limitless potential and simply need the right opportunity to shine.

Focus on Character: Promoting an internal candidate can be a leap of faith. Oftentimes, colleagues struggle to imagine teachers in administrative roles. Rather than worry about "lack of experience," decision-makers should consider character traits. Does this person hold themselves to high expectations? Does this person command the respect of their peers? Does this person build relationships with students? Quite often, the evidence is there. You just need to know where to look.

Contract Concerns: Many districts threaten *"You've signed a contract, you can't leave!"* when employees consider bolting for another job late in the hiring season. The truth is—at least here in Iowa—employees have until June 30th to get out of their contract without facing licensure repercussions. And while it is common to ask exiting employees to pay a fine for rescinding a signed contract, oftentimes these fines pale in comparison to the salary increase the employee will receive in their new position.

To no one's surprise, our administrator accepted the promotion in the nearby district.

Rather than get upset about the situation, I felt at peace knowing this individual was fulfilling their potential by having a greater impact in a larger district.

Furthermore, I felt good knowing I had helped a valued employee reach their leadership potential.

Questions for Discussion:

Reflect: Reflecting on your own experiences, how have you responded when key team members or employees moved on to new opportunities? In what ways have your reactions or actions aligned with the idea of supporting their growth, as described in the chapter?

Apply: How might you adjust your approach to better foster and celebrate the professional development of those around you?

Balance: In what ways might you support and celebrate the professional growth of your team members while also effectively managing the impact of their departure on your organization?

Optimize: Which of the leadership development strategies listed at the end of the chapter can you integrate into your own leadership approach, and how might these strategies enhance the growth and retention of talent within your organization?

Conclusion

"There may be people who have more talent than you, but there's no excuse for anyone to work harder than you."

—Derek Jeter

※ ※ ※

Let me ask you: *How does it end?*

The Ed Leadership Playbook equips you with 30 powerful lessons, your personal playbook for navigating the challenges and demands of educational leadership.

You can close these pages and say *"That was good, I'll have to remember this stuff"* as you place this book back on the shelf and return to everyday life much the same as it was before.

Or, you can close these pages and say *"That was good, let's put these ideas into action"* as you implement your favorite concepts for the purpose of making life better than it was before.

My hope is that you embrace lifelong learning. Read books, reflect on experiences, and seek out mentors. When you come across a golden nugget of truth or quote that changes your perspective, file it away for future use.

In one year, you'll see progress as your influence becomes greater. In five years, you'll notice a separation from your peers. And in ten years, you'll be seen as an expert in your field.

Leadership is a game, and this is your playbook. By putting these lessons into action, I am confident that you will lead your team to victory.

Looking for More?

If you've finished *The Ed Leadership Playbook—30 Lessons for Success* and are hungry for more, visit my website *www.drjared smith.com*. When you get there, check out the following:

Newsletter (drjaredsmith.com/newsletter): My newsletter offers bite-sized pieces of content on leadership, education, and personal growth each week. My goal is not to spam your inbox, but rather to share useful ideas to benefit your life.

Blog (https://www.drjaredsmith.com/articles): If you enjoyed the content shared in these pages, you'll want to check out my full list of blog entries. Each article provides practical insight, advice, and encouragement connected to everyday, real-life experiences.

Speaking (drjaredsmith.com/speaking): Seeing others improve as a result of what they have been taught is highly motivating and brings me great pleasure. I would be honored to educate your audience on any of the principles covered in this book. Visit my website or email me at: *dr.jaredrsmith@gmail.com*.

Podcast (drjaredsmith.com/podcast): The Group Project Podcast shares inspiring interviews from a wide-ranging group of successful individuals—perfect for anyone looking to enhance their professional and personal lives.

Book Summaries (drjaredsmith.com/book-summaries): If you enjoy getting book recommendations, you'll want to check my book summaries collection. I provide three big takeaways and other key ideas on hundreds of books on leadership, education, and personal growth.

About the Author

Dr. Jared Smith is the Superintendent of the Waterloo (Iowa) Community School District. With more than 10,000 students and 1,700 employees, Waterloo is among the 10 largest school districts in Iowa.

Jared has taught and coached at both the middle school and high school levels. Prior to becoming a superintendent, Jared worked as an assistant principal and principal for ten years.

Jared holds a BA in Elementary and Middle Level Education from the University of Northern Iowa, an MS in Educational Leadership from National Louis University, and a PhD in Educational Leadership from Iowa State University.

Jared is an award-winning blogger, professional speaker, adjunct professor, and author of two other books, including the Amazon Best Seller *Turning Points: More Lessons Learned on Leadership, Education, and Personal Growth.*

Thank You

To My Family: For always being my biggest fans and loving me unconditionally.

To My Friends: For giving me honest feedback on the pieces of this book that worked . . . and the pieces of this book that did not.

To the Waterloo Community School Board: For your ongoing support of this book and the work you do for students.

To Waterloo Community Schools and South Tama County Schools Employees: For trusting me to share the ideas outlined in this book—many of which originated in these two districts.

To My Blog Readers: For reading my work and providing feedback; your encouragement provided the motivation needed to complete this book.

To Vicki St. James: For being an amazing editor! For anyone needing a professional editor at an affordable price, visit: *www.stjamesediting.com* or email her at: *vs485539@gmail.com*.

To 1106 Design: Michele DeFelippo, Ronda Rawlins, and the entire team did an amazing job transforming my manuscript into a living, breathing book. Looking to self-publish? I would highly recommend you check out: *https://1106design.com/*.

Endnotes

1. Medina, N. (2014). *Brain rules: 12 principles for surviving and thriving at work, home, and school.* Pear Press.
2. Brown Brené. (2010). *The gifts of imperfection.* Hazelden.
3. Covey, S. (2005). *The 8th habit: from effectiveness to greatness.* New York: Free Press.
4. Nova, A. (2018, March 8). Almost half of professionals lose sleep over work. CNBC. https://www.cnbc.com/2018/03/08/almost-half-of-professionals-lose-sleep- over-work.html
5. Carnegie, D. (1936). *How to win friends and influence people.* New York: Simon and Schuster.
6. Kouzes, J. & Posner, B. (2010). *The truth about leadership: the no-fads, heart-of-the-matter facts you need to know.* San Francisco, CA: Jossey-Bass, A Wiley Imprint.
7. Maxwell, J. (2007). *The 21 irrefutable laws of leadership: follow them and people will follow you.* New York, NY: HarperCollins Leadership.
8. Solomon, L. (2017, Oct. 25) *"Two-Thirds of Managers Are Uncomfortable Communicating with Employees."* hbr.org/2016/03/two-thirds-of-managers-are-uncomfortable-communicating-with-employees.

9. Drazen, L. (2011, July 11). *Americans still lack trust in company management post-recession.* Retrieved from http://www.businesswire.com/news/home-20110711005277-en/Americans-Still-Lack-Trust-in-Company-Management-Post-Recession.

10. Scott, K. (2017). *Radical candor: be a kick-ass boss without losing your humanity.* New York: St. Martin's Press.

11. Horstman, M. (2016). *The effective manager.* Hoboken, New Jersey: Wiley.

12. Ferriss, T. (2017, June 14). *Esther Perel interview | the tim ferriss show (podcast).* YouTube. Retrieved May 24, 2022, from https://www.youtube.com/watch?v=Hu-sCM0eXaw

13. Sinek, S. (2019). *Leaders eat last: Why some teams pull together and others don't.* Penguin Business.

14. Wiseman, L., and S. R. Covey (2017). *Multipliers: How the best leaders make everyone smarter.* HarperBusiness, an imprint of HarperCollinsPublishers

15. Bradley, J. (n.d.). Cisco IBSG Horizons. Retrieved May 24, 2022, from https://www.cisco.com/c/dam/en_us/about/ac79/docs/re/DDC_IBSG-Horizons.pdf

16. Kislik, L. (2022, February 1). *What do newer generations of employees want, and can your business adjust?* Forbes. Retrieved May 24, 2022, from https://www.forbes.com/sites/lizkislik/2022/01/28/what-do-newer-generations-of-employees-want-and-can-your-business-adjust/?sh=573981d12ee0

17. Machiavelli Niccolò. (2014). *The prince.* Penguin Classics, an imprint of Penguin Books.

18. Luna, T., & Renninger, L. A. (2015). *Surprise: Embrace the unpredictable, engineer the unexpected.* Perigee Trade.
19. Goldring, E. (2015). *Making Time for Instructional Leadership* [Scholarly project]. Retrieved from https://www.wallacefoundation.org/knowledge-center/Documents/Making-Time-for-Instructional-Leadership-Vol-3.pdf
20. Steinbach, R. (n.d.). *Employees want feedback—but no one is giving it.* Recruiter.com. Retrieved June 28, 2022, from https://www.recruiter.com/recruiting/employees-want-feedback-but-no-one-is giving it/#:~:text=The%20problem%20is%2C%20employees%20aren,feedback% 20than%20they%20currently%20get
21. Zenger, J., & Folkman, J. (2017, June 27). *The ideal praise-to-criticism ratio.* Harvard Business Review. Retrieved June 28, 2022, from https://hbr.org/2013/03/the-ideal-praise-to-criticism
22. Minshew, K. (2012, July 31). 6 tricks for Better Performance Reviews | Inc.com. Inc. https://www.inc.com/kathryn-minshew/best-practices-for-performance-reviews.html
23. Cross, R. & Parker, A. (2004). *The hidden power of social networks: understanding how work really gets done in organizations.* Boston, Mass: Harvard Business School Press.
24. Brown, B. (2018). *Dare to lead: brave work, tough conversations, whole hearts.* New York: Random House.
25. Murphy, D., & Ginsberg, M. B. (2002, May 1). *How walkthroughs open doors.* ASCD. Retrieved June 7, 2022, from https://www.ascd.org/el/articles/how-walkthroughs-open-doors
26. Goldring, E. (2015). *Making Time for Instructional Leadership* [Scholarly project]. Retrieved from https://www.wallacefoundation

.org/knowledgecenter/Documents/Making-Time-for-Instructional-Leadership-Vol-3.pdf

27. Covey, S. M. R. (2022). *Trust and Inspire: How Truly Great Leaders Unleash Greatness in Others*.

28. Zhenjing G, Chupradit S, Ku KY, Nassani AA, Haffar M. Impact of Employees' Workplace Environment on Employees' Performance: A Multi-Mediation Model. Front Public Health. 2022 May 13;10:890400. doi: 10.3389/fpubh.2022.890400. PMID: 35646787; PMCID: PMC9136218.

29. Hsieh, T. (2013). *Delivering happiness*. Grand Central Publishing.

30. Mann, S. (2017, August). *Advanced Placement Access and Success: How do rural schools stack up?* Retrieved from https://www.ecs.org/wp-content/uploads/Advanced-Placement-Access-and-Success-How-do-rural-schools-stack-up.pdf

31. *Newswire: Consumer trust in online, social and mobile Advertising Grows*. (2012, November 04). Retrieved from https://www.nielsen.com/us/en/insights-article/2012-consumer-trust-in-online-social-and-mobile-advertising-grows/#:~:text=According-20to%20Nielsen's%20latest%20Global-an%20increase%20of%2018%20percent

32. Peek, S. (2020, March 17). *Why employees quit (and how to reduce turnover rates)*. business.com. Retrieved June 7, 2022, from https://www.business.com/articles/reasons-employees-quit/

33. Clifton, J., & Harter, J. K. (2020). *It's the manager: Moving from Boss to coach*. Gallup Press.

34. Caruso, C. (2004, April). *Overtime and Extended Work Shifts: Recent Findings on Illnesses, Injuries, and Health Behaviors.*

Retrieved from https://www.cdc.gov/niosh-docs/2004-143/pdfs/2004-143.pdf

35. Han, F. (2014, December 01). *The ROI of lunch*. Retrieved from https://www.huffpost.com/entry/the-roi-of-lunch_b_5915598

36. Chapman, G. (2015). *The 5 love languages: The secret to love that lasts*. Northfield Publishing.

37. Chapman, G. D., & White, P. E. (2019). *The 5 languages of appreciation in the workplace: Empowering organizations by encouraging people*. Northfield Publishing.

38. Willink, J. (Host). (2015, Dec 31). Jocko & Echo (The Last Hundred Yards [book], Jiu Jitsu, Bosses, Failure) (No. 3) [Audio podcast episode]. Jocko Podcast. Jocko Podcast. https://jockopodcast.com/2015/12/31/jocko-podcast-3-jocko-echo-the-last-hundred-yards-book-jiu-jitsu-bosses-failure/

39. Fried, J., & Heinemeier Hansson, D. (2010). Rework. Crown.

40. Collins, J. (2001). Good to Great. Random House Business Books.

41. Elzinga, D. (2021, August 16). *The biggest lie in HR: People quit bosses not companies*. Culture Amp. Retrieved May 24, 2022, from https://www.cultureamp.com/blog/biggest-lie-people-quit-bosses#:~:text=Our%20data%20showed%20that%20the,12%25%20and%2011%25%20respectively.

42. Collins, J. C. (2001). *Good to great*. Harper Business.